THE BATTLE
FOR
PLANET EARTH

FROM ABRAHAM TO ARMAGEDDON

MIKE RUSS

Mike Russ

Beth Am MESSIAH

**Vision
House**

Santa Ana, California 92705

Scripture text: Holy Bible, New International Version, copyright
© 1978, New York International Bible Society. Used by permission.

The Battle for Planet Earth: From Abraham to Armageddon

Copyright © 1981 by Mike Russ
Twin Peaks, California 92391

Library of Congress Catalog Card Number 81-52373
ISBN 0-88449-076-9

Printed in the United States of America.

For Pam

Acknowledgments

Many thanks to Mal Couch, for showing me the importance of the covenants. Also to my brother, Pat Russ, for many valuable suggestions and additions. To Don Tanner, of the Don Tanner Literary Associates, for his overall editing of the entire manuscript, and to Tom Skinner, who taught me what it means to be a Kingdom citizen. To Rebecca Brooks, for risking life and limb for a footnote.

A special thanks to my parents, Frank and Marjorie Russ, who sacrificed to make my education possible.

Table of Contents

1

Descent Into Madness

"Confidence," someone once observed, "is that feeling you get before you fully understand the problem." And it does seem that the only way to be optimistic about the world is to be completely ignorant of the facts. It doesn't take a genius to realize the world is in a mess. Many people are beginning to wonder if the best way to face the future is to avoid facing it! Like the proverbial ostrich, they consider keeping their heads implanted firmly in the sand.

Yet there is real cause to be optimistic. Despite appearances, world events are not happening at random. They are proceeding along a carefully outlined plan—a design so sure that God has guaranteed its outcome in writing. God's covenanted blueprint for our world is clear, precise, and legally binding. It would be hard to sue God for breach of contract; nevertheless, He has morally bound Himself to several legally drawn contracts to show us that there is hope for our seemingly out-of-control world. But His contracts are not all good news. Situations can worsen before they improve.

Thousands of years ago God's fallen creatures instigated the world's first revolt. This dedicated band of revolutionaries hijacked our planet in mid-flight, took over the captain's chair, and started to run things their own way. In this war against God—a conflict between the superpowers of good and evil—

mankind became the pawn. The results have been painfully obvious—wars, hatred, poverty, bitterness, and despair.

The mutiny is almost complete. Our world is about to escalate the war against God. We are about to witness the infamous battle of Armageddon: all the powers of the universe will collide in one great war to decide who will control this planet and mankind.

But the outcome is not in doubt. God has guaranteed the victory—to Himself and to those who stand with Him.

Recorded in the Bible, God's contracts give us His strategy for regaining control of this rebel planet. God has given the insurgents enough rope to hang themselves, and today we are seeing the gallows under construction. The contract of triumph has been signed in blood.

Trouble in Paradise

There was no light, no sound, no life—only a single cold mass covered with black water in an otherwise empty universe. The Spirit of God hovered expectantly above the water.

Suddenly a voice like a huge waterfall split the emptiness. *"Yehi Or!"* The universe exploded with light. It was the kind of brilliance that no man can describe. It was the radiance of God Himself that flashed through the void of space to illuminate a darkened planet.

God spoke again and again. Gradually the churning mass took shape. The water collected, and dry land appeared. Life abounded. God was pleased, and the heavens resounded with the angels' approval.[1]

But the angels are not singing about Earth anymore. Neither are we. Gone is our Garden of Eden, buried under the rubble of ruin.

The first eleven chapters of Genesis tell how evil was introduced into our once-perfect world by that devious and powerful fallen being, Lucifer, *the Light Bearer*. He is also known as Satan, *the Adversary*.[2] The ancient records say that he was once "perfect in beauty" until pride in his high rank poisoned him. Only one obstacle stood between himself and total control of the universe—a formidable obstacle, indeed. He had set himself against his Creator.

War Between God and Satan

God's war with Satan is mysterious and intriguing. The most painfully obvious fact of the battle is that it concerns us. It is strangely flattering that the Heavenly Heavyweights are at this moment locked into combat over us. We rarely feel that we are worth even a small skirmish in the heavens, much less a full-scale frontal assault among all the heavenly host.

But God does not agree with our low self-esteem and, intriguingly, neither does Satan. One of the few things God and Satan agree on is that we are immensely valuable and important; so much so that all the forces of the universe have their attention centered on this one planet—one of nine in our solar system, tucked away in a corner of the Milky Way, one of thousands of galaxies in the universe. Something crucially important is going on here.

It is strange that Satan's battle with God would even involve us. After all, if the Adversary had some argument with the Creator, it seems they could settle it between themselves, celestial six-guns blazing. But man is both the battlefield and the prize, and this is the key which unlocks the puzzle.

According to Jewish tradition, Satan fell because of man.[3] Angels were God's first created beings. They existed before Earth and witnessed its creation.[4] Satan had the honor of being the chief of the angels, and that made him the most powerful and beautiful creature in the universe.[5]

Then Satan became aware that God intended to create a being who would one day stand above angels and, therefore, above him. That being was man. Even though mankind had a humble beginning, coming from the dust of the ground,[6] it is his destiny to rise above angels.

> Do you not know that the saints will judge [rule] the world? . . . Do you not know that we will judge angels?[7]

Initially this sounds incredible. Angels are extremely powerful. When the prophet Daniel saw one, he fell to his hands and knees, shaking.[8] Normally the first thing angels have to say to a person is, "Don't be afraid." Their splendor is almost terrifying, and it is matched by their power. The prophet Isaiah records how one angel killed 185,000 men in one night—one angel![9]

Yet Scripture says we will one day stand above angels. The metaphor of the caterpillar and butterfly is applied accurately to man. We are in the caterpillar stage, awaiting the glory and splendor that will be ours in the resurrection.

> What we will be has not yet been made known. But we know that when he [Jesus] appears, we shall be like him.[10]

We will one day have the same kind of glory that Jesus had when He rose from the dead. What is in store for us is truly amazing.

But even in the caterpillar stage, we are of a different order from the angels, and their task is to look after us.

> Are not all angels ministering spirits sent to serve those who will inherit salvation?[11]

It must be humbling for angels to serve a creature formed from the ground—a creature that will soon become their master. The drama of man's creation and redemption is a lesson to the angels, a lesson involving humility, love, and trust of their Creator.[12] But humility is not Satan's strong suit; this is where he said, "No." He would not accept second-class status in the heavenlies. Some of the other angels refused, too. Since the time of creation, Satan and his army have tried at every turn to stop God's plans concerning us. As commander-in-chief of the rebel forces, he is continually trying to prevent our salvation and glorification.[13]

Although we cannot say for certain that Satan sinned because of mankind, it is an interesting tradition. We do know that the Scripture says Satan fell because of his pride; he would not humble himself. Instead, he fought to wrest control of the universe from the One who sought his humbling.[14] Rather than serve man, Satan would make man serve him. And so Earth became the battle zone of the universe, and man became the prize.

The winner of this cosmic and spiritual war will rule the universe. The Adversary's determination is to rally the forces of hell and humanity for the great campaign at Armageddon. If God can be defeated there, Satan's scheme for dominion over God, this world, and man would be realized.

Satan's strategy to control our planet can be compared to bacteriological warfare. The Adversary brought into our world a virus that affected the spirit as well as the body. Once man was infected with the microbe of sin, evil rapidly overran the world. The symptoms of spiritual disease were dramatic. Just as the mental patient attacks the doctor who is trying to help him, man rose in a suicidal war against the One who had made him.

The story of Earth's descent into madness is chronicled in the early Genesis stories: Adam and Eve, Noah and the Flood, the Tower of Babel. These accounts show that man's hostility grew in ferocity as the population increased. This pattern continues even today.

War Between God and Man

Humanity's war against God is fought in almost monotonous cycles. The story for each battle is the same. Man starts out in harmony with his Creator; then an insurrection follows. God steps in to restore peace. Satan brings disharmony, and another battle begins.

The first war cycle involving humanity started with the first two people. The "forbidden fruit" which Adam and Eve ate produced a change in their thinking. Immediately their self-perception changed. They saw themselves naked and exposed for the first time.[15] Their attitude toward God also changed. Once they welcomed their walks with God. Now they viewed the Creator as a hostile visitor, and they hid from Him.

Although our first parents fell from innocence, God restored the broken relationship. Yet the mental and spiritual damage they had suffered was permanent. Even worse, their fallen nature was passed genetically from generation to generation. From then on, most of man's spiritual and moral attitudes would be severely warped.

Adam's offspring soon produced a godless society, technically progressive but spiritually dead. As the population increased, man's belligerence intensified and became venomous.

By the time of Noah, God "saw how great man's wickedness on the earth had become, and that every inclination of the thoughts of his heart was only evil all the time."[16] The perverseness of humanity made God sorry that He had ever made man. In all the world God could find only one godly person: Noah. Of all humanity, only Noah's family was spared when God destroyed the world with the Flood.

As the waters receded and the Ark settled on Mt. Ararat, Noah and his family climbed down onto the surface of a ravaged globe. They began their new lives as the only human beings on the face of the planet. It must have looked like a modern science fiction story about a few survivors climbing out of a space capsule at the end of World War III.

The Way We Were

The Flood radically changed the world. Before the deluge, Earth was shielded by a thick layer of water vapor in the atmosphere. This protective "canopy" produced what scientists call a "greenhouse effect" on the planet. The water vapor insulated Earth, providing a uniformly warm climate around the world.[17]

In this kind of world the temperature at the North Pole would be the same as at the equator. Scientists have shown that Earth once had this type of climate by finding ferns and other tropical plants in some very unlikely places—beneath tons of ice in Siberia and in the polar regions. These places, like the rest of Earth, were once tropical paradises.[18]

Since the vapor canopy shielded Earth from the sun's more harmful rays, vegetation was lush and healthy. Plants were so nutritious that they supplied all of man's nourishment, making him vegetarian prior to the Flood.[19]

Many of the sun's rays, such as gamma and x-rays, can cause genetic mutations and play a significant role in the aging process. But since the canopy screened out most of these radiations, people lived for hundreds of years.[20]

But then the water vapor canopy collapsed. It fell to Earth in the form of forty days of rain, bringing with it a universal flood.[21]

With its protective canopy gone, the world went through tremendous changes. Man's lifespan dropped dramatically, until man could expect to live only "three score years and ten."[22] In some parts of the world, life expectancy today is not even that long.

Because vegetation had to exist in a harsher climate, it was no longer nutritious enough to be man's only source of food. Humans, like animals, became carnivorous. Among the changes Noah and his family could expect in the new world was a new menu.

> Everything that lives and moves will be food for you. Just as I gave you the green plants, I now give you everything.[23]

But along with this came a change in man's relationship to the animal kingdom. To keep the animals from helplessly becoming somebody's lunch, God put a fear of man into them.

The fear and dread of you [man] will fall upon all the beasts of the earth and all the birds of the air, upon every creature that moves along the ground, and upon all the fish of the sea; they are given into your hands.[24]

Before the Flood, a person could pick his dinner off a tree. But now he had to work harder for his meals and supplement his diet with meat. Hunting became a dangerous necessity. In the larger animals the fear of man produced outright hostility. Bears and lions suddenly became vicious.

Then another problem challenged Noah's descendants. The animal population increased much more rapidly than the humans. This undoubtedly caused a lot of anxiety, for man was being outnumbered rapidly. An animal population threatened man's existence.[25] Knowing how overwhelming the changes and desolation were, God gave Noah direction for the future.

Then God blessed Noah and his sons, saying to them, "Be fruitful and increase in number and fill the earth."[26]

This command seems simple, even unnecessary. But God had two important reasons for what seemed to be obvious directions. First, He wanted to separate future colonies of man to constrain fighting and wars. He was also concerned that as much land as possible be cultivated quickly so it would not become overgrown and useless.[27]

But the people did not spread out as God had intended. As their numbers increased, they banded together in the Mesopotamian Valley (in present-day Iraq). They organized one unified society to keep from being scattered over the Earth.

Now the whole world had one language and a common speech. As men moved eastward, they found a plain in Shinar [Iraq] and settled there.

They said to each other, "Come, let's make bricks and bake them thoroughly." They used brick instead of stone, and tar instead of mortar. Then they said, "Come, let us build ourselves a city, with a tower that reaches to the heavens, so that we may make a name for ourselves and not be scattered over the face of the whole earth."[28]

Once again, man was raising a clenched fist in God's face. One might think that the Flood would have put a stop to this kind of hopeless nonsense. Yet even after that catastrophic judgment, man's spiritual understanding remained hard and myopic. Instead of curing man's hostility, in many ways the Flood increased it.

The generations after the Flood simply did not trust God. Noah's offspring doubted the goodness of a Creator who had only recently destroyed Earth, and they questioned His motives for wanting them to leave their secure colony. The people were convinced that their safety and prosperity came from the strength of their own society, not from God.

It is not surprising that the people looked upon God's order to blanket the Earth as a cruel attempt to divide and oppress mankind. Mistakenly, they assumed that by building a strong nation and making a name for themselves, they could find security from a hostile world, from the unknown elements of being scattered, and from the God they refused to trust.[29] To "cement" their rebellious decision, they ignored God's order and built a tower in the city of Babel.

Another war cycle had started.

The Babylonian Big Shot

History's first anti-hero, Nimrod, led the Babylonian revolt. The seriousness of his insurrection is reflected even in his name, which means "let us rebel."[30] A strong, smooth-talking leader, this great-grandson of Noah gained his fame from his skill as a hunter.

> Cush was the father of Nimrod, who grew to be a mighty warrior on the earth. He was a mighty hunter before the Lord.[31]

Nimrod's hunting skills were given special attention in Scripture because hunting had only recently been invented. Nimrod was gifted with an ability to understand animals. According to tradition, Nimrod discovered how to domesticate horses and other animals and make them man's servants.[32]

The people, living in constant fear of wild animals, greatly appreciated Nimrod's hunting skills. Naturally they looked to him for protection and guidance. Nimrod made the most of the opportunity. Ancient traditions tell us that he was the first to organize people into fortified communities for protection and security. He was the inventor of organized warfare.[33]

The Midrash (Jewish commentary) on Genesis says he "snared people by his words."[34] Men flocked to him and he became the world's first dictator. But Nimrod wanted more than the allegience of men; he wanted their souls.

> He was powerful in hunting and in wickedness before the Lord, for he was a hunter of the sons of men, and he said to them, "Depart from the judgment of the Lord and adhere to the judgment of Nimrod!"
>
> Therefore it is said, "As Nimrod the strong one, strong in hunting, and in wickedness before the Lord."[35]

The phrase "before the Lord" (Hebrew: *liphne Yahweh*) does not mean that God approved of Nimrod. *Liphne* literally means "to the face of" and can imply a defiant attitude.[36]

Nimrod gained such widespread fame that nearly every culture has some myth or legend about him. His uncanny way with animals gave rise to the myth of the centaur, the half-man, half-horse huntsman that has been immortalized in the astrological sign *Sagittarius*, "The Archer."[37] The weapon often associated with Nimrod is the bow.

In another of the several Greek myths about Nimrod, he is called *Phoroneus,* meaning "The Emancipator" or "Deliverer"— the one who delivered the people from their fears. But this title also has religious significance. From the perspective of those who obeyed God, Phoroneus means "The Apostate" because he "freed" people from their fear of God—the fear which the Bible says is the beginning of wisdom.[38]

The ancient Jewish Talmud—the hallowed, collected writings of the ancient rabbis—says Nimrod "incited the whole world to rebel."[39] Nimrod turned men's minds away from true belief in God. He delivered his subjects from the awe of God and the fear of judgment on sin—a fear that had remained in their minds since the recent deluge.

He convinced people that they could ignore God and still escape His judgment by building a tower. The king of the new world ordered the construction of the Tower of Babel to insure the survival of man against the possibility of another watery judgment. The material used to build the tower, burnt brick covered with tar, was chosen because it was waterproof.[40]

With their "waterproof tower," the Babylonians felt secure—free from the possibility of God's interference. They regarded Nimrod as a savior—not only from a hostile environment, but from the power and authority of God.

Ironically, their efforts were an exercise in futility. God had promised never to flood the world again.[41] But the people refused to take Him at His word.

Nimrod was the first of the antichrists—those who are in league with Satan to place this world permanently under his control. Nimrod is a model of the future Antichrist who will arise just before the second coming of Jesus. It is intriguing that the Book of Revelation pictures the Antichrist arriving on a horse and holding a bow, both of which are symbolic of Nimrod.[42]

Like Nimrod, this world dictator will offer solutions to the pressing problems of society and the environment. He will be so powerful militarily that his followers will think war is now impossible.[43] Under his rule the world will shout "Peace and safety!"[44]

Satan's future friend also will revive Nimrod's Babylonian

religion. The Bible speaks of this religious system, set up in direct opposition to the true worship of God, as "the great harlot."[45]

2
The Great Harlot

Today it seems every airport and tourist center has its collection of religious fanatics buttonholing people for money, selling flowers, or performing an imitation of a Stone Age jam session with bells and drums. Surprisingly, most of these cults have a common heritage in Babylon.

The system of Babylon was called a "mystery" religion because it offered "secret" knowledge of spiritual things. The more a person became involved with the religion, the more he was entrusted with its secrets. The secret of the "mysteries" was to show how one could be "illumined." Such enlightenment came through contact with the spiritual realm. Communication with "spirit helpers," "guides," or "the gods" supposedly enhanced one's knowledge of these mysteries. In reality, these spirit helpers were demons whose task was to draw the initiate deeper into the occult.

Although the Babylonians accepted the idea of one superior god, their religion was polytheistic. Initiates into the "mysteries" made contact with many different "gods." Polytheism was one of the "mysteries." It is not the result of ignorant, superstitious minds. The myths of the gods were "mysteries" that carried deeper meanings, explained only to the initiated.[1]

The "mysteries" taught that ecstasy and asceticism were the vehicles to enlightenment and spirit encounters. Those who practiced the Babylonian religion made use of drugs, "sacred" sex, and meditation with incantations (or "mantras" which repeatedly called out the name of some god) in order to transport themselves into the spirit world.[2]

"Outmoded" ideas like morality or goodness were considered harmful because these were behavior patterns that kept the world in darkness. These restrictions held man in bondage. God-given morals had to be discarded before one could advance in the "mysteries." Sex rituals, both heterosexual and homosexual, were basic to the Babylonian system.[3]

The real purpose of the "mysteries" was to strip the participant of everything that had its source in God or came from His image in man. It was only when one had abandoned everything dealing with God—such as conscience or morals—that he was truly initiated. From Satan's point of view, he was also truly "liberated."

The following story is taken from an ancient Babylonian mystery and is interpreted by a present-day follower of the mysteries. Although it contains many occult overtones, it illustrates this stripping of God-given qualities.

It was the sad time after the death of the fair young god of spring, Tammuz [Nimrod]. The beautiful goddess Ishtar [Nimrod's wife], who loved Tammuz dearly, followed him to the halls of Eternity, defying the demons who guarded the Gates of Time.

But at the first Gate, the guardian demon forced Ishtar to surrender her sandals, which the wise men say symbolizes giving up the Will. And at the second Gate, Ishtar had to surrender her jeweled anklets, which the wise say means giving up the Ego. And at the third Gate she surrendered her robe, which is the hardest of all because it is giving up of Mind itself. And at the fourth Gate, she surrendered her golden breast cups, which is giving up of Sex Role. And at the fifth Gate, she surrendered her necklace, which is giving up the rapture of Illumination. And at the sixth Gate, she surrendered her earrings, which is giving up Magick [*sic*]. And finally, at the seventh Gate, Ishtar surrendered her thousand-petalled crown, which is giving up Godhood.

It was only thus, naked, that Ishtar could enter Eternity.[4]

The enlightenment promised by the Babylonian religion placed the initiate in a state where all actions became "good." Having reached illumination, everything he did was now right; there was no longer the possibility of wrong or evil. He was "above" the rest of ignorant humanity who were still limited by ideas of "right" and "morality." This teaching of rising above a moral code is one of the central tenets of Babylonianism, from which occult or "hidden" sciences spread to Egypt, Greece, and the rest of the world.[5] This same teaching is continued today in many religions.

The following examples are from ancient Hindu scriptures that form the basis for many modern movements, including Transcendental Meditation and Hare Krishna.

One who is not conducted by false ego and whose intelligence is not entangled, even killing in this world, he is not killing; and neither is he bound by such action.[6]

The man who knows me [God] as I am loses nothing whatever he does. Even if he kills his mother or his father, even if he steals or procures an abortion; for whatever evil he does, he does not blanch if he knows me as I am.[7]

This Babylonian anti-morality was popularized by the philosopher Nietzche, who encouraged the development of a "master race" of "supermen" who would have the right to world conquest because of their inner superiority. Their superior wisdom justified whatever methods of conquering they chose. Nietzche's rehash of Babylonianism became the inspiration for such evildoers as Adolf Hitler and Charles Manson.[8]

The Maharishi Mahesh Yogi, the guru of Transcendental Meditation, made the following comment about a character in the Bhagavad Gita.

. . .[He had to] attain a state of consciousness which will justify any action of his and will allow him even to kill in love, in support of the purpose of evolution.[9]

. The Manson Family simply followed Babylonian madness to its logical extreme, and consequently one of the Family members could say, "You really have to have a lot of love in your heart to do what I did to [Sharon] Tate."[10]

Fool's Gold

It is easy to trace the satanic origin of the Babylonian "mysteries." The promise of hidden knowledge is the approach Satan used to entice Eve in Eden. God could not be trusted, the Adversary implied. His ways were keeping her from complete "illumination."

> Now the serpent was more crafty than any of the wild animals the Lord God had made. He said to the woman, "Did God really say, 'You must not eat from any tree of the garden'?"
>
> The woman said to the serpent, "We may eat fruit from the trees in the garden, but God did say, 'You must not eat fruit from the tree that is in the middle of the garden, and you must not touch it, or you will die.' "
>
> "You will not surely die," the serpent said to the woman. "For God knows that when you eat of it your *eyes will be opened, and you will be like God, knowing good and evil.*"
>
> When the woman saw that the fruit of the tree was good for food and pleasing to the eye, and also desirable for gaining wisdom, she took some and ate it. She also gave some to her husband, who was with her, and he ate it. Then the eyes of both of them were opened, and they realized they were naked.[11] (Emphasis added.)

Satan's tactics have not changed in the past few thousand years. All the occult sciences and false religious systems of today have their origin in the temptation of Eve, which later became the foundation of Nimrod's religion.

Nor will Satan change his tactics in the future. The Book of Revelation teaches that Satan's mystery religion will be the main anti-Christian force in the world when Jesus returns. We should expect a revival of secret cults. In fact we are already seeing it with the continuation of mystery groups like the Freemasons, the Rosicrucians, and Transcendental Meditation.

Babylon continues to be the mother of spiritual harlots and abominations. Even the Book of Revelation portrays the Babylonian mystery as a drunken harlot.

The woman was dressed in purple and scarlet, and was glittering with gold, precious stones and pearls. She held a golden cup in her hand, filled with the abominable things and the filth of her adulteries. This title was written on her forehead:

MYSTERY
BABYLON THE GREAT
THE MOTHER OF PROSTITUTES
AND OF THE ABOMINATIONS OF THE EARTH.[12]

Babylon's mysteries glitter like fool's gold with the promise of hidden wisdom, but they are filled with emptiness. Just as Adam and Eve discovered, those who seek such empty promises are left standing naked before God.

Failure to Communicate

The rebellion of Adam and Eve could not be blamed on environment—theirs was perfect. Sin did not come from parental influence or family life-style, for Cain and Abel grew up in the same home, under the same parents. Yet one was good and the other evil.

The Babylonian revolt brought the world into another kind of showdown with its Maker. In many ways, the Tower of Babel was the symbol of man's defiance. Besides its function as the rebels' hope of escape from God, it also was the worship center of pagan mysticism. But God knew it was pointless to destroy man again. Man's contrariness could not be cured by starting over with "good stock." The Flood had proven that no amount of physical coercion or punishment would ever change him. Man was spiritually insane.

Because of man's depravity, God promised to deal differently with His creation.

> Never again will I curse the ground because of man, even though every inclination of his heart is evil from childhood. And never again will I destroy all living creatures, as I have done.[13]

Destroying the Babylonians would not change anything in the long run. Man needed to change from the inside out. Until that happened, his history would be an endless repetition of wars with his Creator. So as Babel was being built, God started a short-term and a long-term plan to deal with the rebels. First He put a stop to the construction.

> But the Lord came down to see the city and the tower that the men were building. The Lord said, "If as one people speaking the same language they have begun to do this, then nothing they plan to do will be impossible for them. Come, let us go down and confuse their language so they will not understand each other."
>
> So the Lord scattered them from there over all the earth, and they stopped building the city. That is why it was called Babel—because there the Lord confused the language of the whole world. From there the Lord scattered them over the face of the whole earth.[14]

In this process God accomplished a number of things. Man was scattered over Earth (as God originally intended) and the communication process was slowed. If the language had not been confused, man's evil would have grown unchecked, and his descent into the occult would have subjected him to all the powers of hell. If those powers were easily available and passed on, man's evil would have grown to unimaginable proportions.

We have seen evidence of this protection of languages in our day. Because of language problems and cultural barriers, it has taken thousands of years for the occultic ideas of Babylon, Egypt, and the East to infiltrate Western life.

There also is a bitter irony to the story of Babel. The people built the city to make a name for themselves, and in this they succeeded. The name Babel means "Confusion," which is what striving against God always produces.

But the confusion of languages was only a temporary solution. The second stage of God's attack went to the heart of the problem. God determined to change man's fallen nature from within and thus regain lordship over His wayward subjects.

This program to reestablish God's Kingdom on Earth is what the rest of the Bible is about. From the end of the story of Babel in Genesis 11 to the last chapter of the Book of Revelation, the Bible reveals God's method for curing man's spiritual strangeness and His strategy for conquering our rebellious planet and reestablishing His Kingdom.

Babel fell; Nimrod failed. Mankind had chosen a place, a man, and had desired a name—all contrary to the will of God. Now God would choose a place and a man: The man, Abram; the place, the land of Israel. And God would promise to that man a "great name." God was about to establish the first of His covenants.

3
Abraham's Battleground

With the Israelis and Arabs peering down their gunsights at each other, a centuries-old feud continues over an ancient sheikh's estate. Each time you visit the gas pumps, you are a victim of this Middle East rivalry.

Incredibly, these enemies are brothers from the same father. Abraham's sons, Ishmael and Isaac, were the fathers of the Arab and Jewish peoples, each of whom claim the covenant promise of God for the Holy Land.

As we watch the awesome contest between these warring brothers from the safety of our homes and television sets, few realize the significance of God's contract with Abraham in today's conflict. This agreement is the guiding force behind world politics and events even today, and it affects every person on this planet. Eventually, the fight over Abraham's contract will draw the whole world into war and bring this age to a fiery climax.

Worldwide Contract

God's contracts encompass nations, kingdoms, the world! All of the past, present, and future is bound in His covenants. Knowing this is the key to understanding the destiny of man.

As God's message to mankind, the Bible is divided according

to His contracts. We organize the written word of God under two main categories, Old Testament and New Testament. The word *testament* is an old English synonym for covenant, or contract. About all we use *testament* for any more is in a "Last Will and Testament," so that word has lost much of its original meaning. When we use the terms *Old Testament* and *New Testament,* we are really saying Old Covenant and New Covenant, or Old Deal and New Deal.

The covenant with Abraham, which predates both the Old and the New Testaments, is the most important piece of legislation that God ever made with man. It forever altered the course of the world.

When Abraham was first contacted by God, he was known as Abram (meaning "great father," or "exalted father"). He was seventy-five years old and extremely rich, but he had no children because his wife, Sarai, was barren (Sarai means "contentious," or "aggravating," which may tell us something about his marriage[1]). It was about 2000 B.C. and Abram and Sarai were living in the city of Haran, which today would be in Syria. It was there that Abram received a long distance call—from God.

> ". . .Leave your country, your people and your father's household and go to the *land* I will show you.
>
> "I will make you into a great *nation* and I will bless you; I will make your name great, and you will be a *blessing.* I will bless those who bless you, and whoever curses you I will curse; and all peoples on earth will be blessed through you."[2] (Emphasis added.)

This pact is deceptively simple. A casual reader could easily miss the amazing importance of the program God started with Abram. The basic parts of the agreement are *land, nation,* and *blessing.* Abram was promised land, abundant offspring to form a nation, and a blessing that would spread around the globe through his seed.

Battle Strategy

God's contract with Abram became the turning point of world history. Before this agreement, man's destiny had been on a downhill slide into Satan's domain. But the covenant with Abram provided humanity with hope and the way to freedom. In the covenant God announced His strategy for battle: He would rescue His rebels and rule over them Himself. God's promises to Abram are a three-pronged attack on Satan, which loosened the death grip he had on the world.

The *land* is significant as God's base of operation; the center of His future Kingdom. The millennial reign of Christ will be from the Holy Land. Abram's *nation* of offspring was destined to be God's army which would retake Earth. The *blessing* that His army would impart would bring a new relationship with God. Those blessed through the covenant would be transformed from bitter enemies into God's people. God would be "their God," and they would be "His people."[3] The blessing was salvation—peace with God. The barriers of hostility would be broken down so that "where He is, there we may be also."[4]

The Abrahamic Covenant is God's master plan for Earth. It is the blueprint for human history and destiny. It also is the backbone of the Bible. From Genesis 12 to Revelation 22, the Bible shows how God is fulfilling His promises to Abram, thus bringing His Kingdom to Earth.

The Promised Land

To many people the "Promised Land" is roughly equivalent to "pie in the sky." Abram knew better. God left little doubt about what He was giving Abram. Appearing to him a number of times, the Lord made the promises more specific each time. After God had called Abram out of Haran down to Canaan (the ancient name for the land of Israel), He gave specific instructions, mapping out the boundaries of the Promised Land.

> ". . .Lift up your eyes from where you are and look north and south, east and west. All the land that you see I will give to you and your offspring forever.

> "I will make your offspring like the dust of the earth, so that if anyone could count the dust, then your offspring could be counted.

> "Go, walk through the length and breadth of the land, for I am giving it to you. . . .To your descendants I give this land, from the river of Egypt to the great river, the Euphrates."[5]

The Promised Land was the sweep of the Mediterranean coast extending from the Euphrates River on the north, down to the Nile delta on the west.[6] God confirmed those boundaries hundreds of years later when He told Moses that the western border of the land was the Red Sea.[7] Because the Red Sea and the Nile delta line up on the same geographical parallel, either one was considered the boundary. The inland borders were given later as Abram's heirs were about to receive their inheritance.[8]

In the lower half of Israel, the land extended from the west Mediterranean to the Jordan. This included all of the west bank of the Jordan, presently occupied by Israel, which is so volatile an issue in the Middle East today.

The full extent of the Promised Land encompasses much more land area than people usually associate with the name Israel. Today it would include the nations of Israel, Lebanon, and half of Syria, as well as the Sinai and the west bank of the Jordan.

Long-Term Lease

It is impossible to get a longer property lease than the one Abram received from the Lord. The contract was an everlasting agreement.

> "I will establish my covenant as an everlasting covenant between me and you and your descendants after you for the generations to come, to be your God and the God of your descendants after you.

"The whole land of Canaan, where you are now an alien, I will give
as an everlasting possession to you and your descendants after you;
and I will be their God."[9]

Some people running around in theological circles would like
to limit Abram's land lease. The word *everlasting* (*olam* in
Hebrew) does not always mean "forever," they argue. This is
true. In Exodus 21:2-6, the word applies to the span of a man's
life. But when *olam* is used for future promises or commands, it
means "as long as the present order of things lasts."[10]

When God says a promise will last *olam,* it means that it will
continue as long as the people involved in the promise, or as long
as the earthly order, lasts. If the promise is for one person, it will
last "all his days," as in the Exodus 21 passage. Because the
agreement is for Abram and all future generations of his offspring, it will endure as long as his descendants survive—which
will be at least as long as Earth exists.

But there is one condition. Some of God's contracts include a
clause that could nullify the covenant in the event of disobedience.

"And if at another time I announce that a nation or kingdom is to
be built up and planted, and if it does evil in my sight and does not
obey me, then I will reconsider the good I had intended to do for
it."[11]

Applying this to the nation of Israel, whose chief talent seems
to be disobedience, it seems that she is on the short end of the
contract. But, as we shall see, the pledge of the New Covenant is
that Israel will be given a new heart toward God. An obedient
Israel will enjoy the fulfillment of God's promises.

Abram's lease is still in effect.

Abram or Arab?

Abram's heirs only once controlled the full extent of the
Promised Land, and then for just a brief time under King

Solomon about 980 B.C. Since the land was given to Abram and company forever, its other occupants are only renters. According to the prophet Ezekiel, the territory will belong to Israel again.[12] Imagine the changes that will have to occur in the Middle East before that can happen!

This divine right is a motivating force behind many religious Jews so adamant about keeping the Sinai and the west bank of the Jordan. Many in modern Israel do not concern themselves with the Abrahamic Covenant, however; theirs is an emotional attachment to the land. Still others await the Messiah to reclaim the Promised Land for Israel. Yet the policy of the Israeli government is greatly influenced by this Covenant—even to the brink of war and beyond.

One need not look past the front page of the newspaper to realize that the Arabs feel quite differently about this. They consider *themselves,* not the Jews, the true heirs of Abram and therefore the rightful recipients of the covenant. But to settle the argument that is about to plunge the world into Armageddon, we must revisit Abram.

4

Cutting the Covenant

Ten years after God promised Abram that he would be the father of a great nation, all he had to show for it was a crowd of hired servants, a herd of camels, and two place settings at the family table.

Getting older by the minute (at eighty-five it probably feels like you really do get older by the minute), and still having no children, Abram thought God had put him on "hold." He was becoming depressed. So God appeared to him again to say that everything was still "go."

> . . . "Do not be afraid, Abram. I am your shield, your very great reward."
>
> But Abram said, "O Sovereign Lord, what can you give me since I remain childless and the one who will inherit my estate is Eliezer of Damascus?"
>
> And Abram said, "You have given me no children; so a servant in my household will be my heir."
>
> Then the word of the Lord came to him: "This man will not be your heir, but a son coming from your own body will be your heir."[1]

For most of us, just hearing God speak would leave us

speechless. But Abram was made of sterner stuff. He wanted to get right down to business, especially since God had made the same promises before and nothing had happened. Abram was a little depressed here, and like all of us, he wanted backup. Promises were nice, but let's see some collateral. Abram wanted the agreement in writing.

> He also said to him, "I am the Lord, who brought you out of Ur of the Chaldeans to give you this land to take possession of it."
>
> But Abram said, "O Sovereign Lord, how can I know that I will gain possession of it?"
>
> So the Lord said to him, "Bring me a heifer, a goat and a ram, each three years old, along with a dove and a young pigeon."[2]

When God asked for the animals, Abram knew just what to do. It was a common practice in those days to seal agreements in blood.

> Abram brought all these [animals] to him, cut them in two and arranged the halves opposite each other; the birds, however, he did not cut in half.[3]

The making of a contract was gruesome. The animals were cut in half and spread apart so that the halves formed an aisle. Participants in a covenant walked together between the animal parts.

This ceremony had a dual meaning. On the positive side, it was a symbol of unity. Walking between the parts of the same animal meant that those who had once been divided over an issue were now joined in agreement.

Negatively, it was a blood covenant bearing serious consequences. Tiptoeing through the entrails carried with it a curse. The cut-up animals were a grisly reminder of what would happen to the covenantor or his animals if he later decided to break the contract.[4]

Vultures and Visions

Abram arranged everything—no easy job, considering the size of a three-year-old heifer. Imagine his excitement as he waited for God to come down and walk between the animals with him! But God didn't show up. Abram waited all day and into the night. In the meantime, the carcasses were attracting every buzzard for a hundred miles, and Abram spent the day chasing them away.

> Then birds of prey came down on the carcasses, but Abram drove them away.
>
> As the sun was setting, Abram fell into a deep sleep, and a thick and dreadful darkness came over him.[5]

At dusk Abram collected an unscheduled forty winks (probably because of exhaustion), and God took this opportunity to give him a vision of the future. The delay was prophetic, indicating that it would be many years before the covenant they were about to make would be completely fulfilled. In the vision, Abram was told why it would take so long. He was shown a dismal period of his offspring's future, which filled him with a "thick and dreadful darkness."

> Then the Lord said to him, "Know for certain that your descendants will be strangers in a country not their own, and they will be enslaved and mistreated four hundred years. But I will punish the nation they serve as slaves, and afterward they will come out with great possessions.
>
> "You, however, will go to your fathers in peace and be buried at a good old age. In the fourth generation your descendants will come back here, for the sin of the Amorites has not yet reached its full measure."[6]

This prophecy saw fulfillment when the Israelites spent four hundred years of slavery in Egypt. True to God's word, the Exodus began with Israel in possession of Egypt's great riches.[7]

The Amorites were the people then living in Canaan. Their religious ceremonies consisted of Babylon's "sacred" prostitution and human sacrifice. In worship to Molech, the fire god, they burned their firstborn children alive. God planned for the Israelites to enter the Promised Land when the perversion of the Amorites was at its height because He intended to use Israel as an instrument of justice.

An Offer He Couldn't Refuse

After the vision, God signed the contract with Abram.

> When the sun had set and darkness had fallen, a smoking fire pot with a blazing torch appeared and passed between the pieces. On that day the Lord made [lit. "cut"] a covenant with Abram and said, "To your descendants I give this land, from the river of Egypt to the great river, the Euphrates."[8]

It is crucial to understand what took place. The cutting of the covenant is the bedrock of the Bible, of world history, and of prophecy. With Abram out of commission, God made the covenant walk *alone.* This is highly significant because anyone who walked between the parts was bound by the covenant. In this case God walked alone, in the symbol of smoke and fire (which He would later use to guide Israel through the desert). This meant that the contract was unilateral—one-sided. Its fulfillment would depend entirely on God, not on Abram or his offspring.

If Abram had been with God in the covenant walk, he would have been responsible to uphold his end of the deal. If he had failed, the covenant would have been void, and God could have called the whole thing off. Instead, no matter what would happen to Israel in the future, Abram's descendants would always be assured of their place in the covenant. God took it upon Himself to guarantee its fulfillment. It was a deal Abram couldn't turn down.

If You Can Measure the Heavens

Today, many believe that Israel has been rejected from the covenant because of her disobedience, especially in rejecting the Messiah. But that is not true. The fulfillment of the contract did not, and does not, depend upon Israel's obedience. God said Israel would remain His covenant people despite their rebellion.

> This is what the Lord says: "Only if the heavens above can be measured and the foundations of the earth below be searched out will I reject all the descendants of Israel because of all they have done."[9]

But this did not mean that Israel could get away with sin. God has always punished His people for their sin, but He has never rejected the Jews as His covenant people.

> ". . .They will pay for their sins because they rejected my laws and abhorred my decrees. Yet in spite of this. . .I will not reject them or abhor them so as to destroy them completely, breaking my covenant with them. I am the Lord their God."[10]

How does this reconcile with Jeremiah 18:9,10, which says that God will nullify His promises to those who disobey? Because the Covenant with Abram was one-sided, the agreement would be fulfilled by God's power, not man's. Under the New Covenant, based on Abram's agreement, God promised to draw the people back to obedience. Because of this, Israel's temporary and recurrent disobedience would not nullify the agreement, and God would remain true to His principles.

"No Help Needed"

After the contract cutting, Abram and Sarai eagerly awaited their first child. Again, nothing happened. They panicked.

Did they understand God correctly? After all, they were old and Sarai was still barren. Perhaps God expected them to use their own ingenuity. Maybe God only helps those who help themselves. Abram would still be the father of the child, even if someone other than Sarai were the mother, they reasoned.

Sarai found the likely candidate—Hagar, her servant girl. Sarai probably did not have to twist Abram's arm very hard to make him agree. The child conceived of Abram and Hagar was Ishmael, his heir-apparent. Not until the boy was a teenager and Abram was ninety-nine did God tap on Abram's tent again. He told Abram that he did not need his help in getting things done. Abram had jumped the gun. It was now time for him to receive his true heir.

During this visit, God's first objective was to give Abram and Sarai their new names. Abram, "Exalted Father," became *Abraham,* "Father of Nations." More dramatic was the change in "Contentious." Sarai became *Sarah,* "Princess."[11] (Isn't it amazing what God can do with our cranky personalities?)

> Abram fell facedown, and God said to him, "As for me, this is my covenant with you: You will be the father of many nations. No longer will you be called Abram; your name will be Abraham, for I have made you a father of many nations. I will make you very fruitful; I will make nations of you, and kings will come from you. I will establish my covenant as an everlasting covenant between me and you and your descendants after you for the generations to come, to be your God and the God of your descendants after you. The whole land of Canaan, where you are now an alien, I will give as an everlasting possession to you and your descendants after you; and I will be their God."
>
> God also said to Abraham, "As for Sarai your wife, you are no longer to call her Sarai; her name will be Sarah. I will bless her and will surely give you a son by her. I will bless her so that she will be the mother of nations; kings of peoples will come from her."[12]

Judging from his reaction, Abraham was not exactly a giant of the faith at this point.

Abraham fell facedown; he laughed and said to himself, "Will a son be born to a man a hundred years old? Will Sarah bear a child at the age of ninety?"

And Abraham said to God, "If only Ishmael might live under your blessing!"[13]

Abraham was a practical man. He already had a son. Why not let *him* be the heir? Ishmael's birth may not have been completely kosher, but why not make do with him? Let Hagar's child receive God's blessing and be heir to the covenant.

God's answer is crucial. It is still ringing in the ears of Arabs and Jews today. God told Abraham, "Yes and no." Yes, Ishmael would be blessed; no, he would not inherit the covenant.

Then God said "Yes, but your wife Sarah will bear you a son, and you will call him Isaac [meaning "He laughed"]. I will establish my covenant with him as an everlasting covenant for his descendants after him.

"And as for Ishmael, I have heard you: I will surely bless him; I will make him fruitful and will greatly increase his numbers. He will be the father of twelve rulers, and I will make him into a great nation. But my covenant I will establish with Isaac, whom Sarah will bear to you by this time next year."[14]

Like Father, Like Sons

True to God's promise, Ishmael had twelve sons who settled "in the area from Havilah to Shur, near the border of Egypt."[15] This is in Arabia today. Living in Arabia, Ishmael's offspring became the seed of the Arab peoples. Moslem history still traces many of the Arab tribes back to Ishmael's sons.[16]

From the beginning, these people "lived in hostility toward all their brothers," a conflict that rages even today in the Middle East. Ishmael's sons seem to have inherited the disposition of their father. Before Ishmael was born, God gave a prophecy about him to his mother Hagar.

"He will be a wild donkey of a man; his hand will be against everyone and everyone's hand against him, and he will live in hostility
toward all his brothers."[17]

Often that prophecy comes to mind when I drive up to the gas
pump. It's interesting how even the picture of an Arab oil sheikh
has become such an object of hatred in recent times.

Who's Got the Blessing?

Born one year after God's visit, Isaac was the start of
Abraham's nation, Israel. Years later, Isaac had twin sons. The
first was born with much hair, so they called him "Hairy." In
Hebrew, it's Esau. The second had his hand on his brother's heel
as they were delivered, so he was named "Heel Catcher," or
Jacob.

According to the culture of the day, Esau was the natural
recipient of the birthright; but by divine forethought, Jacob fell
heir to the covenant instead.[18] And so the covenant passed from
Abraham to Isaac to Jacob.

One night an angel appeared to Jacob, who wrestled with the
alien all night until the angel blessed him. Impressed with
Jacob's perseverance, the messenger of God gave him the title,
"Israel," meaning "fighting with God," or "having power with
God."[19] In doing so, the angel named Jacob after his grand-
mother Sarai. The names Sarai and Israel both come from the
Hebrew word *sarah*, meaning "to persevere" or "strive."[20] The
Lord saw in Jacob the character of his grandmother Sarai.

Israel's twelve sons shared in the covenant, passing their
blessing on to the tribes that they fathered.[21] These tribes
eventually became the nation Israel. Israel became Abraham's
promised nation through whom God would bless the world, making the territory it occupies the rightful inheritance of the
children of Abraham, Isaac, and Jacob.

The name Israel is ironically prophetic. The nation named

"fighting with God" has been doing just that throughout most of its history. It is still at odds with Him in its rejection of Jesus. Nonetheless, what God did for Sarai, He can do for Israel—and will. According to the prophets, Israel will experience a complete change of heart toward God and His Messiah when the nation joins the New Covenant.

What's in a Name?

The book of Genesis ends in Egypt with the death of Joseph, Jacob's eleventh son. But before his passing, Joseph gave us a list of Abraham's heirs.

> Joseph said to his brothers, "I am about to die. But God will surely come to your aid and take you up out of this land [Egypt] to the land he promised on oath to Abraham, Isaac and Jacob."[22]

Israel often calls God, "the God of Abraham, Isaac and Jacob," which is another way of saying, "the God of the covenant." Even God Himself used this formula to identify Himself when He appeared to people, as in this famous scene with Moses.

> . . .Moses saw that though the bush was on fire it did not burn up. So Moses thought, "I will go over and see this strange sight—why the bush does not burn up."
>
> When the Lord saw that he had gone over to look, God called to him from within the bush, "Moses, Moses!"
>
> And Moses said, "Here I am."
>
> "Do not come any closer," God said. "Take off your sandals, for the place where you are standing is holy ground." Then he said, "I am the God of your father, the God of Abraham, the God of Isaac and the God of Jacob."[23]

Here we have it from the Ultimate Authority that the covenant passed from Abraham to Isaac to Jacob. With such immutable proof, one wonders how this fact can be in dispute.

5

The Muslim Messiah?

One need only tune into the latest news to know that all this is not music in Arab ears. The idea of Jewish divine right is repulsive to them.

The genesis of the argument is found in the religious bond between the countries of the Middle East. Almost universally Moslem, their peoples are guided by the Koran, the holy book of the Islamic religion.

In Arabic the word *Islam* means "the surrender [to God]," and *Muslim* or *Moslem* means "one who has surrendered." A Moslem, then, is one who has *Islamed*, or surrendered, to God through the teachings of Mohammed in the Koran.[1]

The "bible" of Islam, the Koran was written by Mohammed around A.D. 600. This makes Mohammed a new kid in town when it comes to self-proclaimed prophets. Genesis, written by Moses about 1400 B.C., was two thousand years old, and Christianity had been around six hundred years by the time Mohammed came on the scene.

According to the story, Mohammed was seeking truth while fasting and meditating in a cave during the now sacred month of Ramadan (July/August in the Moslem lunar calendar). He was visited by an angel who identified himself as Gabriel. This "Gabriel" told Mohammed that he had been chosen as God's messenger.

After the Ramadan revelation, Mohammed claimed to have had a number of visions which were given to him during trances. Written down and collected, these revelations became the Koran, or "The Reading."[2] The Koran is mostly concerned with rules for moral living and warnings against idolatry, but the foundation of its teaching is directly opposed to the Bible.

Too Many Hands in the Cookie Jar

For an up-and-coming prophet to make a splash in the religious world, he must establish some authority and status to back up his teachings. Mohammed found much of his clout in Ishmael. Like most Arabs, Mohammed claimed to be a direct descendant of Abraham's first son.[3]

He went back to Genesis and rewrote the story, making Ishmael Abraham's primary heir. Ishmael was not excluded from the covenant, as the Bible says. Instead, he and Isaac were actually co-heirs of Abraham. According to Mohammed, the covenant belongs to the Ishmaelites as much as it does to the Jews.

In the Bible, the God of the covenant is "the God of Abraham, Isaac and Jacob." In the Koran, Mohammed did some reshuffling of the covenant heirs.

> Were ye present when death came to Jacob; when he said to his sons, "What will you worship after me?"
>
> They said, "We will worship thy God, the God of Abraham and Ishmael and Isaac; One God and unto Him we have surrendered."[4]

Not only has Mohammed included Ishmael in the covenant formula, he also has Jacob's sons promising to "surrender" to God. By a simple Arabic word play, they are pledging to be good Moslems ("Surrenderers").

Mohammed said Ishmael was never rejected, but was totally acceptable to God.

And make mention in the scripture of Ishmael. He was a keeper of his promise, and he was a messenger of Allah, a prophet. He enjoined upon his people worship and almsgiving, and he was acceptable in the sight of his Lord.[5]

Moslems believe that God exalted Ishmael far above Isaac. It was Ishmael, not Isaac, who was Abraham's promised miracle child. Ishmael was the child Abraham almost sacrificed (the Bible says it was Isaac); and it was Ishmael who, along with Abraham, was the foundation of Islam—the "pure" religion of Abraham. Mohammed said Ishmael and Abraham built the Moslem temple at Mecca and placed inside a sacred black meteorite stone which all Moslems hope to kiss at least once in their lives during their required pilgrimage to Mecca.[6]

Ishmael kept the "pure faith" of Abraham and passed it down to his offspring, but Isaac's children "wandered astray," according to Mohammed. Even though Mohammed paid lip service to Isaac's original place in the covenant, he taught that Jews have lost their inheritance and forfeited any claim to Abraham. This also is true of Christians, whom Mohammed called "blasphemers." As the only true followers of Abraham's religion, Moslems should now be considered the only true heirs of Abraham. But this privilege is not just reserved for Arabs. All Moslems, Arab and non-Arab, share the "claim" to Abraham.

O People of the Scripture [Jews and Christians]! Why will you argue about Abraham when the Torah [the Old Testament] and the Gospel [the New Testament] were not revealed till after him? Have you no sense?

. . .Abraham was not a Jew, nor yet a Christian, but an upright man who had surrendered [in Arabic: *Muslim*]. He was not of the idolators.

Those of mankind who have the best claim to Abraham are those who have followed him and this prophet [Mohammed] and those who believe.[7]

Mohammed used the same word play here to make Abraham a Moslem, thus "proving" that Islam predates both Judaism and Christianity, and making Moslems more deserving of the covenant. Mohammed wanted the authority of Abraham behind his teachings, and it was all the better if he could steal it in the name of God.

God promised Abraham, "All the peoples on earth will be blessed through you."[8] The Bible says this blessing comes through Jesus, the descendant of Isaac and Jacob.

Mohammed claimed that the blessing comes through the one special offspring of Ishmael—Mohammed. Islam teaches that the promises made to Abraham did not look forward to Jesus, but to Mohammed, whom Moslems call, "Son of Ishmael."[9]

It is not surprising that Mohammed had to deny clear Biblical teachings to support his deception. In order to exhalt himself above Jesus, Mohammed demoted the Son of God to the rank of mere mortal. Jesus was simply one of many prophets, not God in any sense.

> They say, "Be Jews or Christians, then you will be rightly guided." Say unto them, "Nay, but we follow the religion of Abraham, the upright. He was not of the idolators."
>
> Say, "We believe in Allah and that which was revealed unto Abraham and Ishmael and Isaac and Jacob and the [twelve] tribes and that which Moses and Jesus received and that which the prophets received from their Lord. *We make no distinction between any of them* and unto Him [Allah] we have surrendered."[10] (Emphasis added.)
>
> Christ the son of Mary was no more than an apostle; many were the apostles that passed away before him.[11]

Notice how often Mohammed stresses the point that Abraham "was not of the idolators." Mohammed taught that it was idolatry to say God had "partners," such as a Son. He said the Biblical doctrine of the Trinity "joined gods with God" and is blasphemy. To believe that Jesus was the Son of God (as He said He was) was an unforgivable sin by Mohammed's teaching.

> O People of the Book [the Bible]! Commit no excesses in your religion, nor say of God aught but the truth.

> Christ Jesus the son of Mary was [no more than] an apostle of God. . .so believe in God and His apostles. Say not "Trinity": desist! It will be better for you. For God is One God: glory be to Him. Far exalted is He above having a son.[12]

> God forgives not [the sin of] joining other gods with Him; but He forgives whom He pleases other sins than this. One who joins other gods with God has strayed far, far away.[13]

> They do blaspheme who say, "God is Christ the son of Mary."

> But said Christ, "O Children of Israel! Worship God, my Lord and your Lord."

> Whoever joins other gods with God, God will forbid him the Garden, and the Fire will be his abode. There will for the wrong-doers be no one to help.

> They do blaspheme who say God is one of three in a Trinity. For there is no god except One God. If they desist not from their work [of blasphemy], verily a grievous penalty will befall the blasphemers among them.[14]

But the Bible looks at things quite differently.

> No one who denies the Son has the Father; whoever acknowledges the Son has the Father also.[15]

> The Father judges no one, but has entrusted all judgment to the Son, that all may honor the Son just as they honor the Father. He who does not honor the Son does not honor the Father who sent him.[16]

Mohammed carried his blasphemy to the point of saying that Jesus predicted Mohammed's coming and even called him a messenger of God.

> And when Jesus son of Mary said, O Children of Israel! I am a
> messenger of Allah unto you, confirming that which was [revealed]
> before me in the Torah [the Old Testament], and bringing good
> tidings of a messenger who comes after me, whose name is "The
> Praised One."[17]

The name "Praised One" in Arabic is *Ahmed,* the root of the
name Mohammed.[18] Ironically, Jesus probably did predict
Mohammed's coming, but in a far different way than the author
of the Koran supposed.

> At that time if anyone says to you, "Look, here is the Christ!" or,
> "There he is!" do not believe it. For false Christs and false prophets
> will appear and perform great signs and miracles to deceive even
> the elect—if that were possible. See, I have told you ahead of time.[19]

Jesus said false prophets like Mohammed will be judged by
their own words.[20] In the Koran, Mohammed asked a question
that will be very hard for him to answer in the judgment.

> Who does greater wrong than he who invents a lie against Allah
> when he is summoned unto Al-Islam [the Surrender]?[21]

To paraphrase Mohammed's question, "Who does greater
wrong than he who invents a lie against God when he is
summoned to the truth?"

Irresistible Forces and Immovable Objects

As we have seen, the Middle East conflict is the battle for
Abraham's covenant. It is the controversy of Jew versus Moslem,
Genesis versus the Koran, Jesus versus Mohammed, God versus
Satan. Both sides are fighting for what they believe is theirs by
divine right. It is a conflict not easily solved.

The current ferment sweeping the world's nine hundred
million Moslems raises the specter of a united Pan-Islamic
crescent of nations stretching from North Africa to Indonesia. In
terms of global politics, the consequences could be staggering.

Involved are one-fifth of Earth's population and Middle East oil.

The political power of the Koran has become frighteningly obvious with the recent overthrow in Iran. And now that same religious zeal—along with Pakistan's nuclear capability—has added to the potential for global holocaust. News analysts are calling Pakistan's potential weapon the "Islamic Bomb" because Pakistan's religious ties to the Moslem block could make the bomb available to all of them.

While it would be inaccurate to consider these Moslem nations united in policy and goals (some of them don't even like each other, as the war between Iran and Iraq has demonstrated), they do share one critical attitude—a denial of Israel's territorial claims, and even her right to exist. These countries present a united block against Israel, and they are willing to use oil to blackmail the world into isolating Israel. In seizing power in Iran, the Ayatollah Khomeini vowed, "Today Iran, tomorrow Palestine."[22]

The 1980s will witness increasing panic as people and nations go to extremes in seeking security. Our world is too sophisticated to build waterproof shelters like the Tower of Babel, but the tower-building mentality is alive and well. A sound economy and abundant oil have replaced the brick and tar, but there is a tower, nonetheless. Camouflaged by a dozen satanic counterfeits, the deception of Babylon is everywhere. But surely and inexorably, God is revealing Himself as the God of Abraham, Isaac, and Jacob.

He is a master strategist. Using this ancient controversy and Israel as an irritant, He is focusing world attention on the Middle East. There He will gather for a destined showdown the armed forces of a world enchanted by Babylon.

One day soon world history will reach its climax in the Valley of Jezreel below Mt. Megiddo, from which the term *Armageddon* is derived. The Bible calls this "the valley of decision," where the Creator will confront a world that no longer recognizes Him.

Proclaim this among the nations:
    Prepare for war!
Rouse the warriors!
    Let all the fighting men draw near and attack.
Beat your plowshares into swords
    and your pruning hooks into spears.

Let the weakling say,
    "I am strong!"
Come quickly, all you nations from every side,
    and assemble there.
Bring down your warriors, O Lord!

Let the nations be roused;
    let them advance into the Valley of Jehoshaphat,
for there I will sit
    to judge all the nations on every side.
Swing the sickle,
    for the harvest is ripe.
Come, trample the grapes,
    for the winepress is full
    and the vats overflow—
So great is their wickedness!

Multitudes, multitudes
    in the valley of decision!
For the day of the Lord is near
    in the valley of decision.
The sun and moon will be darkened,
    and the stars no longer shine.
The Lord will roar from Zion
    and thunder from Jerusalem;
    the earth and the sky will tremble.
But the Lord will be a refuge for his people,
    a stronghold for the people of Israel.

Then you will know that I, the Lord your God,
    dwell in Zion, my holy hill.
Jerusalem will be holy;
    never again will foreigners invade her.[23]

But because Israel is ultimately on the winning side doesn't mean that everything she does *now* is right. An unbelieving nation, Israel is still in rebellion against God and His Son. Israel is fighting for a land rightly hers, but her methods for occupation are not necessarily always right. Christians walk a tightrope in their attitude concerning Israel—one which Paul summarized.

> As far as the gospel is concerned, they are enemies on your account; but as far as election is concerned, they are loved on account of the patriarchs [Abraham, Isaac, and Jacob], for God's gifts and his call are irrevocable.[24]

We need to view Israel as God sees her—beloved because of her place in the covenant, but—like the rest of the non-Christian world—at war with God over her rejection of Jesus. We must not curse the seed of Abraham, for God said He would curse those who curse Abraham.[25] That grim promise applies both to nations and to individuals. Yet we need not ignore our difference with Judaism. We can support Israel, but not to the point of "Israel, right or wrong."

Strange as it may sound, Israel is destined to become a Christian nation. When she enters the New Covenant, Israel will finally be brought to faith in Messiah Jesus. She will then take her full and rightful place in the covenant and receive all its promises.

To understand the enormity of this miracle, we must examine another contract between God and Israel—the Old Covenant.

6

"Whom God Has Joined Together..."

The Jews are both a miracle and a mystery.

For almost two thousand years they have kept their national identity, even though they had no homeland for most of that time. No other people in history have been able to exist for more than a few generations without their own country (when is the last time you met a Serbian, much less a Babylonian?). The Jews have exerted an influence on history which belies their numbers.

Making up only one-half of one percent of the world's population, they have received fifteen percent of the world's Nobel prizes.[1] Albert Einstein, Sigmund Freud, Karl Marx (and Groucho), George Gershwin, Arthur Rubinstein, Bob Dylan, Paul Newman, Henry Kissinger, Neil Simon, Henry Winkler (the "Fonz"), and Vidal Sassoon are a few of the many Jewish people who have shaped our world. Despite their small numbers, the Jews are constantly in the forefront of world affairs.

Yet no other people have been so despised, so persecuted, so feared, so barbarously treated. Hatred pursues them. Scarcely a generation ago, Hitler's Third Reich eliminated one-third of world Jewry. Every Jewish family lost at least one relative.

It is as if a curse follows Abraham's seed. They are always in the spotlight, but it is that spotlight which brings both acclaim and acrimony.

The Jewish people are in the limelight for a reason—God put

them there. He made a covenant with Israel which placed them on display. The Old Covenant is the story of Israel on stage before the world. She became a gigantic magnet, attracting world attention to herself and to her God. In the process this God-rejecting world is being drawn together for its encounter with the Creator.

Israel in Egypt

The account of the Old Covenant begins with Israel's transformation from a small nomadic clan (Jacob's family) to a mighty nation. One might expect that such a change involving God's chosen people would be suitably holy and miraculous. Actually, it started with a lot of jealousy and back-stabbing.

Jacob's sons had just read the Canaanite best-seller of 1900 B.C. *Looking Out for Number Echad* (that's "one" for modern readers) and decided they were fed up with the favoritism their father showed Joseph, his eleventh son. Joseph's brothers sold him to a caravan of slave traders who took him to Egypt. There Joseph spent many years as a slave and a prisoner until it was discovered that he could interpret dreams. Through this ability, God promoted Joseph to the position of prime minister of Egypt—second only to Pharaoh himself.

After his meteoric rise to power, Joseph was reunited with his family, who had sold him down the Nile River. They were understandably nervous about seeing him again, but from 20/20 hindsight, Joseph was able to see God's hand in all that had happened.

> . . .do not be distressed and angry with yourselves for selling me here, because it was to save lives that God sent me ahead of you. . .to preserve for you a remnant on earth and to save your lives by a great deliverance.
>
> So then, it was not you who sent me here, but God.[2]

The immediate danger from which Joseph saved his family was seven years of famine. By interpreting Pharaoh's prophetic dreams, Joseph had prepared Egypt for the shortage. Her vast food storehouses kept Israel's family secure. But Egypt saved Israel from a far more insidious enemy—a serpentine plot to destroy the tiny nation.

Guess Who's Coming to Dinner

Genesis 38 is a strange chapter of the Bible. It seems to be out of place. Standing in the middle of Joseph's story, it seems to be unrelated to Joseph's troubles. Genesis 38 is about Judah, Joseph's oldest brother. It is filled with immorality and deceit and shows how far the spiritual life of Abraham's seed had fallen. Even worse, Abraham's offspring had begun to intermarry outside his family line.

For any other people, this would not be a big deal. But God had great plans for Abraham's descendants, and now the tiny nation was about to be assimilated into the different cultures around them. Israel was in danger of ceasing to exist as a unique people. Jacob's sons were throwing themselves and all future generations of mankind into great danger without realizing it. They had lost sight of their uniqueness, of their role in establishing the Kingdom of God, and of their place in destroying the satanic world system.

In order to save the nation and His budding Kingdom, God sent Israel to Egypt by way of Joseph's good fortune there. Because Egypt was extremely racist, it was the perfect place to send Jacob and the clan. The Egyptians thought they were the gods' gift to mankind, and they kept their society carefully segregated. It was definitely taboo for an Egyptian to marry with any of the "lower" races.[3] With Israelites forbidden to marry Egyptians, Egypt became a natural guard to preserve Abraham's nation.

Egypt was like a mother's womb. Israel entered it as a seed and there grew and developed for four hundred years until Abraham's people had become a nation of more than two million. That means each family had an average of six children, a common tradition in those days (Jacob had twelve sons and a daughter).

Soon the twelve sons of Israel had developed into the twelve tribes of Israel. The Egyptians did not look kindly upon this threatening growth of foreigners. Considering the Israelites a social, political, and national security risk, the Egyptians did the "expedient" thing. They enslaved the Jewish people, stripping them of all civil rights, and sentenced any male born to an Israelite to immediate death. This was the first time a nation attempted what Hitler later would call "the final solution to the Jewish problem."

God would not allow the extermination of His chosen. He appointed Moses to rescue His people and bring the newly formed nation back to the land given to them as heirs of Abraham, Isaac, and Jacob.

Although the Egyptians despised the Israelites, they wanted to keep them around for cheap labor. It was not a red-letter day on Pharaoh's calendar when Moses told him that God wanted His people out. Pharaoh tried to prevent it, but God's persuasion was quite dramatic. By the time Moses had called down the ten plagues, Egypt was in chaos and Pharaoh's advisers were begging him to let Israel go—anywhere!

The Birth of a Nation

The suffering of Israel and the plagues that followed were like a mother's birth pangs. Egypt was the mother about to give birth to a nation that had been formed within her. Israel was born in one day as God parted the Red Sea, and the twelve tribes crossed over into freedom for the first time in four hundred years. God went before His rescued nation in the form of a fiery cloud and led them down to Mt. Sinai for a truly incredible encounter.

At Sinai God revealed His astonishing plan: Israel was to be a kingdom of priests—a nation completely made up of God's representatives. The Israelites were to be God's spokesmen to a lost and rebellious world. They would be the ones to reach the world and help to bring it out of its satanic fog.

> You yourselves have seen what I did to Egypt, and how I carried you on eagles' wings and brought you to myself. Now if you obey me fully and keep my covenant, then out of all the nations you will be my treasured possession. Although the whole earth is mine, you will be for me a kingdom of priests and a holy nation.[4]

Actually, this was a plan for global evangelism. God would speak through Israel to the world, and Israel would be God's instrument to win it back.

God's main purpose for the Old Covenant at Sinai was to prepare a people He could use to set up His kingdom. Because Israel had to be prepared morally and spiritually, God gave a series of laws (summed up in the Ten Commandments) and established a system of animal sacrifices.

The laws and sacrifices worked together. If an Israelite failed in any law, he was required to offer a sacrifice to "atone" for, or to "cover," his sin. God was training the people to understand forgiveness. Animal sacrifices prepared Israel for the ministry of the Messiah who would later come as "the lamb of God who takes away the sin of the world."[5]

Moses received the laws and sacrificial instructions from God and brought them back to the people. These were the terms of the covenant that they were about to make with God. When Moses came down from the mountain, the actual signing of the contract got under way.

> When Moses went and told the people all the Lord's words and laws, they responded with one voice, "Everything the Lord has said we will do." Moses then wrote down everything the Lord had said.
>
> He got up early the next morning and built an altar at the foot of the mountain and set up twelve stone pillars representing the twelve tribes of Israel. Then he sent young Israelite men, and they offered

burnt offerings and sacrificed young bulls as fellowship offerings to the Lord.

Moses took half of the blood and put it in bowls, and the other half he sprinkled on the altar. Then he took the Book of the Covenant [containing the laws and regulations] and read it to the people. They responded, "We will do everything the Lord has said; we will obey."

Moses then took the blood, sprinkled it on the people and said, "This is the blood of the covenant that the Lord has made with you in accordance with all these words."[6]

As we saw with Abraham's contract, the way a covenant was "cut" is extremely important. Abraham's contract was a one-sided agreement because only God walked between the animal parts. The Sinai covenant had a slightly different form. Instead of walking between the parts, the participants were sprinkled with the blood of the animals. This signified that they were bound in blood by the covenant.

The crucial difference between these covenants is that the Sinai contract was two-sided. The Old Covenant was a voluntary agreement between two parties, God and Israel. Both sides joined in the confirming sacrifice. God was represented by the altar; the people represented themselves. Since the people entered the agreement, they would be responsible if they later broke it.

For Better or for Worse

At Mt. Sinai, God married Israel.[7] From now on they would be partners for better or for worse. Picturing the Old Covenant as a marriage contract is the best way to understand its implications fully. God had irrevocably linked Himself to a nation, and its people were irrevocably linked to God. This is the incredible secret behind the Old Covenant and the key to understanding how it would work.

God wanted Israel to be His mouthpiece in the world, but the way He was to speak was much louder than words. By drawing attention to her, God was going to show the world that Israel was His wife. But the way Israel would attract attention was up to her. If the people were faithful to the covenant, God would bless them more than any nation on Earth. By this the world would realize that Israel was established by God and would even be afraid of her.

> If you fully obey the Lord your God and carefully follow all his commands I [Moses] give you today, the Lord your God will set you high above all the nations on earth. All these blessings will come upon you and accompany you if you obey the Lord your God:
>
> You will be blessed in the city and blessed in the country. . . .You will be blessed when you come in and blessed when you go out [this Hebrew figure of speech means that everything they did would be blessed]. . . .The Lord will send a blessing on your barns and on everything you put your hand to. The Lord your God will bless you in the land he is giving you.
>
> The Lord will establish you as his holy people, as he promised you on oath, if you keep the commands of the Lord your God and walk in his ways.
>
> Then all the peoples on earth will see that you are called by the name of the Lord, and they will fear you.[8]

This was only half the story.

Israel could keep the covenant or break it, but they could not walk away from it. Because the Old Covenant was bilateral, Israel would fulfill her role of showing the way to God even if she later broke the contract. She would be God's witness in the world either voluntarily—by following the Law—or involuntarily—by forsaking the Law.

If the people chose to follow the Law, God would bless them amazingly. If they disobeyed, Israel would be the most cursed nation ever to live on the face of the planet. The world would know that God was dealing with the nation because of her great good fortune, or great misfortune. Either way, Israel would point the way to God and so fulfill her part of the covenant.

> However, if you do not obey the Lord your God and do not carefully follow all his commands and decrees I am giving you today, all these curses will come upon you and overtake you:
>
> You will be cursed in the city and cursed in the country. . . .You will be cursed when you come in and cursed when you go out. The Lord will send on you curses, confusion and rebuke in everything you put your hand to, until you are destroyed and come to sudden ruin because of the evil you have done in forsaking him. The Lord will plague you with diseases until he has destroyed you from the land you are entering to possess. . . .
>
> The sky over your head will be bronze, the ground beneath you iron. . . .The Lord will cause you to be defeated before your enemies. . .and you will become a thing of horror to all the kingdoms on earth.[9]

If Israel decided to break the contract, their curses would cause the world to ask, "Why do such awful things always happen to the Jews?" Their misfortune would be their witness. Like the blessings, the curses would have to be so great that the world would attribute them to God and not to bad luck.

"Choose Life!"

God was careful to define the full implications of the covenant. One can almost hear Him pleading with the people.

> See, I have set before you today life and prosperity, death and destruction. For I command you today to love the Lord your God, to walk in his ways, and to keep his commands, decrees and laws; then you will live and increase, and the Lord your God will bless you in the land you are entering to possess.
>
> But if your heart turns away and you are not obedient, and if you are drawn away to bow down to other gods and worship them, I declare to you this day that you will certainly be destroyed. You will

not live long in the land you are crossing the Jordan to enter and possess.

This day I call heaven and earth as witness against you that I have set before you life and death, blessings and curses. Now choose life, so that you and your children may live and that you may love the Lord your God, listen to his voice, and hold fast to him. For the Lord is your life, and he will give you many years in the land he swore to give to your fathers, Abraham, Isaac and Jacob.[10]

The giving of the Old Covenant ends with a prophecy that is both ominous and hopeful.

When all these blessings and curses I have set before you come upon you and you take them to heart wherever the Lord your God disperses you among the nations, and when you and your children return to the Lord your God and obey him with all your heart and with all your soul according to everything I command you today, then the Lord your God will restore your fortunes and have compassion on you and gather you again from all the nations where he scattered you . . . he will bring you to the land that belonged to your fathers, and you will take possession of it. . . .

The Lord your God will circumcise your hearts and the hearts of your descendants, so that you may love him with all your heart and with all your soul, and live.[11]

Since God knows the end from the beginning, He knew that Israel would eventually break the covenant and experience both its blessings and curses. For this reason He comforted the people even before the curses had come upon them. He wanted to assure them that He would always be their covenant partner. Even after Israel had been scattered over the Earth, in fulfillment of one of the curses, God would not reject His people. He promised to regather and reestablish their nation. He also promised to correct the rebellious attitude that had caused them to break the covenant. The people would experience a complete change of heart.

The miracle of a changed life is actually part of the New

Covenant that God would later make with Israel (and also the Gentiles). This was the first promise of that coming covenant.

7

Blessings and Curses—
A Two-Edged Sword

Israel got off to an incredibly bad start. The generation that "cut" the Old Covenant at Sinai never made it to the Promised Land.

As they approached the land, they sent twelve spies out on reconnaisance. The report was not encouraging. Canaan was well defended and many of the Canaanites were large people ("We seemed like grasshoppers"). Two of the spies, Joshua and Caleb, tried to tell the people that God would give them what He promised despite outward appearances.

But the people were scared and refused to enter their inheritance. They told Moses it was "because of the kids."[1]

God was furious that Israel could be so faithless after He had just reduced Egypt, the most powerful nation on Earth, to ruins so they could escape. Couldn't He do the same with these Canaanites? God declared that none of those who had escaped Egypt would enter the Promised Land, except "the kids" and the two faithful spies.

Not one of you will enter the land I swore with uplifted hand to make your home, except Caleb son of Jephunneh and Joshua son of Nun.

As for your children that you said would be taken as plunder, I will bring them in to enjoy the land you have rejected. But you—your bodies will fall in this desert. Your children will be shepherds here for forty years, suffering for your unfaithfulness, until the last of your bodies lies in the desert.

For forty years—one year for each of the forty days you explored the land—you will suffer for your sins and know what it is like to have me against you.[2]

After the first generation had died, God gathered the nation at the Jordan River (the boundary of Abraham's property) and repeated the Old Covenant with them. This covenant rerun is found in the Book of Deuteronomy, which means "Second Law." It contains the same Old Covenant, but as repeated to the second generation. This second covenant was made about 1400 B.C., forty years after the first. After the contract cutting, Joshua led the people into their land.

The first enemy stronghold they came to was Jericho, the most highly fortified city in Canaan. The battle strategy was unique—trumpet blasts and shouts conquered the city. Israel learned a bitter lesson at Jericho. They could have had the land forty years earlier had they only trusted God and not panicked over the "looks of things."

The Blessing

Israel had no human government because God was her King. He wanted to rule over the people personally. Israel was a true theocracy, ruled by God. Human leadership came through priests and judges. The judges were the spiritual and military leaders who guided one or more of the twelve tribes during times of emergency.

During the time of the judges, the spiritual life of Israel degenerated severely. The people no longer viewed themselves as unique and could not relate to an invisible King. The majority of Israel worshiped Canaanite idols which they could see and touch.

Wanting to be like other nations with a human king, the

people asked Samuel, the last of the prophet-judges to appoint a ruler.

> But when they said, "Give us a king to lead us," this displeased Samuel; so he prayed to the Lord. And the Lord told him, "Listen to all the people are saying to you; it is not you they have rejected as their king, but me. As they have done from the day I brought them up out of Egypt until this day, forsaking me and serving other gods, so they are doing to you. Now listen to them, but warn them solemnly and let them know what the king who will reign over them will do."
>
> [Samuel then told them how their future king would tax them and force their children into government service.]
>
> "When that day comes, you will cry out for relief from the king you have chosen, and the Lord will not answer you in that day."
>
> But the people refused to listen to Samuel. "No!" they said. "We want a king over us. Then we will be like all the other nations, with a king to lead us and to go out before us and fight our battles."
>
> When Samuel heard all that the people said, he repeated it before the Lord. The Lord answered, "Listen to them and give them a king."[3]

Samuel appointed Saul king over a united Israel. He started out as a good man, but eventually he fell into serious disobedience. Because of his insolence, God rejected Saul and appointed David in his place.

This did not go over well with Saul, who had no intention of giving up the throne. David spent the first few years of his "reign" being chased all over the Judean countryside by Saul's troops. Not until Saul was permanently removed in a battle with the Philistines did David ascend to the throne.

David was a good king—"a man after God's own heart."[4] He had some notable failures, such as his infamous adultery with Bathsheba, but unlike Saul, David had the character to admit his sin and seek God's forgiveness. Because he kept his heart toward God, the Lord made Israel one of the world's most power-ful nations (as the Old Covenant had promised). God also promised David that the Messiah—the one who would bring in the Kingdom of God—would be born in David's family line.

David's son Solomon took over after him. Solomon was David's son through Bathsheba, which is a testimony to God's forgiveness. He took Israel to the heights promised in the Old Covenant. Because of Solomon's faithfulness, Israel became the most blessed nation on Earth. Other nations streamed to her for trade and counsel.

> King Solomon was greater in riches and wisdom than all the other kings of the earth. The whole world sought audience with Solomon to hear the wisdom God had put in his heart. Year after year, everyone who came brought a gift—articles of silver and gold, robes, weapons and spices, and horses and mules.[5]

One of Solomon's visitors was the famous Queen of Sheba (in Arabia). In her visit we can see the Old Covenant in operation. God had so blessed Israel that the queen knew immediately that Israel's God was the true God.

> When the Queen of Sheba saw all the wisdom of Solomon and the palace he had built, the food on his table, the seating of his officials, the attending servants in their robes, his cupbearers, and the burnt offerings he made at the temple of the Lord, she was overwhelmed.
>
> She said to the king, "The report I heard in my own country about your achievements and your wisdom is true. But I did not believe these things until I came and saw with my own eyes. Indeed, not even half was told to me; in wisdom and wealth you have far exceeded the report I heard. How happy your men must be! How happy your officials, who continually stand before you and hear your wisdom! Praise be to the Lord your God, who has delighted in you and placed you on the throne of Israel. Because of the Lord's eternal love for Israel, he has made you king, to maintain justice and righteousness."[6]

It seemed as if Israel were going to end up on the winning end of the Old Covenant. She was a powerful witness for God and, because of this, Solomon was given the entire portion of Abraham's promised land. He ruled over "all the kingdoms from the River [Euphrates] to the land of the Philistines [to the Mediterranean], as far as the border [lit. 'river'] of Egypt."[7] Solomon was the first Israelite king to rule the entire Promised Land.

He was also the last.

Solomon's power eventually went to his head. Ignoring clear prohibitions of the covenant, he took hundreds of wives and concubines, many of whom were pagan. The results were disastrous.

> As Solomon grew old, his wives turned his heart after other gods, and his heart was not fully devoted to the Lord his God, as the heart of David his father had been. He followed Ashtoreth the goddess of the Sidonians, and Molech the detestable god of the Ammonites. So Solomon did evil in the eyes of the Lord. . . .[8]

Because he was David's son and because of his earlier faithfulness, God allowed Solomon to live out his life as king. But the kingdom would be taken from Solomon's son, even though he would be allowed to rule over his own tribe of Judah.

After Solomon's death, his son Rehoboam took the throne. Soon a revolt split Israel. The ten tribes in the north separated from the two southern tribes, and Israel became a divided nation—never to be united until the regathering of 1948.

The ten northern tribes banded together under the name Israel. The southern territory, made up mostly of the tribe of Judah, became the nation of Judah.

The End of Israel

The northern kingdom started out bad and grew worse. One of the first things King Jeroboam did was to set up golden calf worship at the town of Bethel. He was afraid that if the people continued to worship at the temple of Jerusalem, in the territory of Judah, they would rejoin Judah and revolt. This paganistic, rival religion not only kept the people away from Jerusalem, but it angered God.

God sent many prophets to Israel to remind the people of the covenant and the curses. Yet king after king continued Jeroboam's idolatry. When the people refused to listen to the prophets, they received their first taste of the Old Covenant curses.

At Mt. Sinai, God had given Israel this grisly picture of what would happen.

> If in spite of these things you do not accept my correction but continue to be hostile toward me, I myself will be hostile toward you and will afflict you for your sins seven times over. And I will bring the sword upon you to avenge the breaking of the covenant. When you withdraw into your cities, I will send a plague among you, and you will be given into enemy hands. When I cut off your supply of bread, ten women will be able to bake your bread in one oven, and they will dole out the bread by weight. You will eat but not be satisfied. . . .

> You will eat the flesh of your sons and the flesh of your daughters. I will destroy your high places [pagan temples], cut down your incense altars and pile your dead bodies on the lifeless forms of your idols, and I will abhor you. . . .

> I will lay waste the land, so that your enemies who live there will be appalled. I will scatter you among the nations and will draw out my sword and pursue you. Your land will be laid waste, and your cities will lie in ruins.[9]

Israel learned that God's warnings do not grow impotent with age.

> Some time later [about 850 B.C.], Ben-Hadad king of Aram [Syria] mobilized his entire army and marched up and laid seige to Samaria [the capital of Israel]. There was a great famine in the city;

the seige lasted so long that a donkey's head sold for eighty shekels of silver [about two month's wages] and a fourth of a cab [½ pint] of seed pods for five shekels.

As the king of Israel was passing by on the wall, a woman cried to him, "Help me, my lord the king! . . . This woman said to me, 'Give up your son so we may eat him today, and tomorrow we'll eat my son.'

"So we cooked my son and ate him. The next day I said to her, 'Give up your son so we may eat him,' but she had hidden him."[10]

Yet after Israel had been reduced to such terrible conditions, their repentance lasted only a short time. They quickly reverted to paganism. One king would be faithful, and the very next would be rebellious. The people simply followed their examples.[11]

Finally God had enough. In fulfillment of the covenant warnings, He removed Israel from the land. In 721 B.C. Assyria invaded Israel and took most of the people captive.

The Lord warned Israel and Judah through all his prophets and seers: "Turn from your evil ways. Observe my commands and decrees, in accordance with the entire law that I commanded your fathers to obey and that I delivered to you through my servants the prophets."

But they would not listen and were as stiff-necked as their fathers, who did not trust in the Lord their God. . . .They forsook all the commands of the Lord their God and made for themselves two idols cast in the shape of calves, and an Asherah pole [a phallic symbol used for fertility rites]. They bowed down to all the starry hosts, and they worshiped Baal. They sacrificed their sons and daughters in the fire. They practiced divination and sorcery and sold themselves to do evil in the eyes of the Lord, provoking him to anger.

So the Lord was very angry with Israel and removed them from his presence. Only the tribe of Judah was left.[12]

When the ten tribes of Israel went into captivity, they became the "Ten Lost Tribes." They are called "lost" because history seems to lose track of them after this point. But the Bible says that at least some members of each of these groups returned to Israel after the collapse of Assyria.[13]

Modern cults have made the "Lost Tribes" into everything from the American Indians to the Anglo-Saxon race, but historical evidence indicates that most of the exiles stayed in Assyria (which later became the region of Armenia) or became the beginning of Europe's large Jewish population.[14] Biblical prophecies say that all the tribes will be regathered and reunited in the last days.[15] Even today the "lost" tribes are not lost. Many modern-day Jews still carry their tribal identity in their last names (Levi, Benjamin, Simon, etc.).

Judah in Ruins

With the northern kingdom, Israel, in captivity, Judah was alone in Abraham's inheritance. This was when the word *Jew* became synonymous with *Israelite*, since Judah was the only representative of Israel.

Judah was a little better off than her northern relatives. Every now and then she had a king who wanted to make the people destroy their idols and act as a "covenant partner."

Kings like Josiah and Hezekiah tried to get Judah to shape up, but—like Israel—the people repented for only a short while, then returned to the more spectacular pagan rituals.

God used the same early warning system with Judah—the prophets. They told Judah that she would share Israel's fate if the people did not return to the covenant. The message fell on deaf ears.

In 605 B.C. Babylon invaded Judah and took captive those who were considered valuable: the rich, the young, and the gifted (like the prophet Daniel). Judah became a vassal state of Babylon. The freedom-loving Jews rebelled under the

Babylonian yoke—something the Babylonians took a very dim view of. And in 587 B.C. Babylon again invaded Judah, destroyed Jerusalem and the temple, and took most of the people captive. Thus, the seed of Abraham was banished from the land, and Israel was in ruins.

Back to Jerusalem

Babylon did for Israel's religious life what Egypt had done for its physical existence. Babylon saved the covenant religion from extinction by crushing paganism out of Israel.

Babylonian society was totally immersed in idolatry and pagan "mysteries" that dated back to Nimrod. God threw Israel into the cesspool of Satan's counterfeits. It's amazing how terrible our sins look when we see others commit them. And from their Babylonian perspective, the people could see how they had broken the Sinai Covenant, and they purged themselves of paganism.

With the temple gone, the synagogue became the local meeting place and source of strength. Just as He had promised in the Old Covenant, God did not forget His people in Babylon.

> If they will confess their sins and the sins of their fathers—their treachery against me and their hostility toward me, which made me hostile toward them so that I sent them into the land of their enemies—then when their uncircumcised hearts are humbled and they pay for their sin, I will remember my covenant with Jacob and my covenant with Isaac and my covenant with Abraham, and I will remember the land. . . .
>
> When they are in the land of their enemies, I will not reject them or abhor them so as to destroy them completely, breaking my covenant with them. I am the Lord their God.[16]

Through the prophets Isaiah, Jeremiah, Ezekiel, and Daniel, God promised that they would return to the land and rebuild their cities.

Daniel was given some of the most amazing prophecies in the Bible. He foresaw the rebuilding of Jerusalem and the coming of the Messiah.[17] But during the next five hundred years of waiting, Israel would be ruled by a succession of four Gentile world powers.

By the time Jerusalem had gathered fifty years of dust on its ruins, Babylon had fallen to the Persians and the new emperor, Cyrus, allowed the Jewish exiles to return. Out of the more than one million who had been taken captive, only fifty thousand chose to go. The rest felt more comfortable in Babylon.

Most of the Jews did not understand the importance of their mission in the Promised Land. Those who did, returned to Jerusalem to begin the huge task of rebuilding the nation.

True to Daniel's prophecy, three great Gentile kingdoms— Babylon, Persia, and Greece—came and went over Abraham's land. It was during the Roman Empire, Daniel's fourth Gentile kingdom, that the time was fulfilled for the coming of the Messiah.

The Messiah

He was in the world, and though the world was made through him, the world did not recognize him. He came to that which was his own, but his own did not receive him.[18]

Jesus' relationship with His fellow Jews was always tenuous at best. The first sermon He delivered so enraged His audience that they took Him outside town to kill Him (an episode that should comfort every first-time Bible teacher).[19]

By the time Jesus came on the scene, the Jewish religion had become cold and formal. The strict observance of rituals had become the measure of one's righteousness. Jesus tried to show that the law and its rituals were vehicles to lead the people into a love relationship with God and man.

One of the teachers of the law came . . . he asked him, "Of all the commandments, which is the most important?"

"The most important one," answered Jesus, "is this: 'Hear, O Israel, the Lord our God, the Lord is one. Love the Lord your God with all your heart and with all your soul and with all your mind and with all your strength. The second is this: Love your neighbor as yourself.' There is no commandment greater than these."

"Well said, teacher," the man replied. "You are right in saying that God is one and there is no other but him. To love him with all your heart, with all your understanding and with all your strength, and to love your neighbor as yourself is more important than all burnt offerings and sacrifices."

When Jesus saw that he had answered wisely, he said to him, "You are not far from the kingdom of God."[20]

In God's eyes, sacrifices were like Band-Aids—they covered wounds. What God wanted was obedience. It was disobedience that made sacrifices for sins necessary. But the people had made the sacrifices the most important part of the law. They were more concerned with an insurance for forgiveness than with obedience.

Jesus' words were acid when aimed against the religious leaders who had buried the real law under tons of traditions— traditions which had, in effect, cancelled out the original intent of the law.

Jesus replied, "And why do you break the command of God for the sake of your tradition? For God said, 'Honor your father and mother,' and 'Anyone who curses his father or mother must be put to death.'

"But you say that if a man says to his father or mother, 'Whatever help you might otherwise have received from me is a gift devoted to God,' he is not to 'honor his father' with it. Thus you nullify the word of God for the sake of your tradition.

"You hypocrites! Isaiah was right when he prophesied about you:
'These people honor me with their lips,
but their hearts are far from me.
They worship me in vain;
their teachings are but rules taught by men.' "[21]

Obviously Jesus was a threat to the religious establishment of His day. The leaders were vehement in their opposition to Him because Jesus had the nerve to claim authority above the Law and even above the temple—the house of God!

> I tell you that one greater than the temple is here. If you had known what these words mean, "I desire mercy, not sacrifice," you would not have condemned the innocent. For the Son of Man is Lord of the Sabbath.[22]

Admittedly these were hard words to swallow, but Jesus backed them up with amazing miracles to show the truth of what He was saying: He really was the Son of God who had been given "all authority in heaven and on earth" by His Father.[23]

> If I had not done among them what no one else did, they would not be guilty of sin. But now they have seen these miracles, and yet they have hated both me and my Father. But this is to fulfill what is written in their law; "They hated me without reason."[24]

The religious leaders could not deny the signs, but neither would they accept Jesus' claims. They took the only other option open to them and attributed Jesus' power to Satan.

> Then they brought him a demon-possessed man who was blind and mute, and Jesus healed him, so that he could both talk and see. All the people were astonished and said, "Could this be the Son of David [the Messiah promised to David]?"

> But when the Pharisees heard this, they said, "It is only by Beelzebub, the prince of demons, that this fellow drives out demons."[25]

Knowing that the leaders had rejected Him, Jesus realized it was just a matter of time before the people would follow suit. Israel was about to make the biggest mistake of her life. She was about to call for the crucifixion of her only hope, for Jesus was the One Who was to establish the Kingdom of God. Also, the people were about to call down on themselves the curses of the Old Covenant.

> As he approached Jerusalem and saw the city, he wept over it and said, "If you, even you, had only known on this day what would bring you peace—but now it is hidden from your eyes. The days will come upon you when your enemies will build an embankment against you and encircle you and hem you in on every side. They will dash you to the ground, you and your children within your walls. They will not leave one stone on another, because you did not recognize the time of God's coming to you."[26]

> For this is the time of punishment in fulfillment of all that has been written. How dreadful it will be in those days for pregnant women and nursing mothers! There will be great distress in the land and wrath against this people. They will fall by the sword and will be taken as prisoners to all nations.[27]

Here Jesus was repeating what God had told the nation 1,400 years before when they "cut" the Old Covenant with Him.

> The Lord will bring a nation against you from far away, from the ends of the earth, like an eagle swooping down, a nation whose language you will not understand, a fierce-looking nation without respect for the old or pity for the young. . . .

> They will lay siege to all the cities throughout your land until the high and fortified walls in which you trust fall down.[28]

The Romans

The Romans were a stern, cruel people. Many of the Roman governors in Judea, Samaria, and Galilee (Israel was now divided) were openly anti-Semitic and they delighted in provoking the Jews. Their rule was often oppressive.

The Jews were always suspect because their religion prevented them from worshiping the emperor. To the Jews, mighty Rome was just another Gentile nuisance.

The mistrust was mutal. In A.D. 19, Emperor Tiberius ordered all Jews out of Rome because he considered them subversives. Tiberius also revoked some of the self-governing privileges granted to other Roman provinces and subjects.[29] As a result, hatred fermented against the cursed, pagan overlords. In A.D. 66, thirty-three years after the crucifixion of Jesus, Israel revolted.

The rebels were tremendously outnumbered. Only 23,000 civilians stood against 60,000 of Rome's finest. But with a cause and purpose, the Jews fought like fanatics, holding out for four years against the Roman war machine.[30]

In A.D. 69, the rebels overpowered the Roman garrison at Jerusalem, took over the city, and prepared to defend it against the inevitable Roman siege.

The Curse

The Lord will afflict you with madness, blindness and confusion of the mind.[31]

The story of the battle for Jerusalem is like black comedy. Some of it would almost be funny were it not so tragic.

The Jewish defenders were convinced that Jerusalem could never be taken again by the heathen. The prophet Zechariah had seen a vision of the battle for Jerusalem which will happen at the end of our age. Zechariah saw God rescue the city from the Gentiles gathered against it. The battle was the climactic event of the age because it led to the downfall of the heathen and the coming of the Kingdom of God.[32]

For the Jewish rebels, the gathering of Rome against Jerusalem surely signaled the end of the age and the coming of the Messiah. God would rescue His city at the critical moment and set up the Kingdom.

The rebels were so sure of their invincibility that they started fighting among themselves to see "who would be the greatest in the Kingdom." Three factions in the city fought among themselves. Incredibly, they burned each other's food supplies that had been stored for the siege.[33]

While the Jews busily burned their own food, the Romans were building a siege wall around the city.

The rebels waited in vain for God's intervention. Jesus foresaw this tragedy and told His listeners about it.

When you see Jerusalem surrounded by armies, you will know that its desolation is near.[34]

Remembering Jesus' words, the Christians in the city fled and were spared its gruesome fate.

Josephus, the Jewish historian, was an eyewitness to the fall. He recorded its desolation with grisly detail. The siege did not last long, as sieges go. It was all over in six months.

Without food the Jews soon began to starve. They resorted to cannibalism. At night they tried to gather food outside the city walls. Sometimes as many as five hundred a night were caught by Romans and crucified in public view. There were so many crucifixions that the Romans ran out of wood. Out of boredom, the soldiers experimented with different shapes of crosses and invented unusual ways of hanging bodies on them. Approximately 600,000 bodies, victims of starvation, were thrown out of the city gates. More than one million Jews perished in the battle for Jerusalem.[35]

Ironically the city fell to the Romans in A.D. 70 on the 9th of Ab (August/September), which was the same day Jerusalem fell to the Babylonians 600 years earlier. God was making the lesson hard to miss.

Altogether 97,000 Jews were taken captive. Most were sent to the Egyptian salt mines or sold as slaves. With the market glutted, the price of a slave fell to that of a horse. Many could not find buyers.[36]

But the people had been warned in the covenant.

> The Lord will send you back in ships to Egypt on a journey I said you should never make again. There you will offer yourselves for sale to your enemies as male and female slaves, but no one will buy you.[37]

The Romans thought it best to keep the Jews humiliated and powerless. Nearly all self-governing privileges were abolished for the Jews. The half-shekel tax the Jews paid for the upkeep of the temple was now used by the Romans to support the temple of Jupiter Capitolinus in Rome.[38]

Later the Emperor Hadrian tried to eliminate the Jewish religion by forbidding circumcision, the study of the Torah (the Old Testament), and the observance of the Sabbath and other Biblical feasts.

These outrages proved too much for the Jews who, amazingly, decided once again to throw off the yoke of the Roman demon, sixty-two years after the fall of Jerusalem. This second revolt started in A.D. 132 under the military leadership of Simon bar-Kochba. Rabbi Akiba, the most famous religious leader of the day, publicly proclaimed bar-Kochba the Messiah and deliverer of Israel.

Their previous defeat had only heightened the messianic hopes of the people. The prophecies said the Messiah would come during the "great and terrible day of the Lord."[39] So, the further down the Jews were pushed, the higher their hopes reached for their long-awaited—and long-rejected—Messiah.

The followers of bar-Kochba fought ferociously, thinking they were divinely protected. The fight lasted three-and-a-half years and nearly succeeded in gaining Israel's independence. But in the end, the relentless, methodical Roman war machine triumphed.

Israel in Ruins

This time the Roman punishment sought out the heart of the "Jewish problem." Since Jerusalem was the center of Judaism, the Romans made it a crime punishable by death for a Jew even to enter Jerusalem—except for one day a year, the 9th of Ab. After paying heavy bribes, the people were allowed to weep at the Wailing Wall, the last remnant of the temple, on the anniversary of the destruction of both temples.

On the temple grounds the Romans erected a sanctuary to Jupiter and altars to Venus and Bacchus. They also changed the name of the Promised Land to "Palestine," after Israel's ancient enemies, the Philistines.[40]

A thousand villages lay in ashes after the bar-Kochba revolt. The land was decimated by the wars with Rome. An eyewitness, Josephus, chronicled the sorrowful events.

> And truly, the very view itself was a melancholy thing, for those places which were before adorned with trees and pleasant gardens were now a desolate country in every way and its trees were all cut down.
>
> Nor could any foreigner that had formerly seen Judea and the most beautiful suburbs of the city [Jerusalem] and now saw it as a desert, but lament and mourn sadly at so great a change. For the war had laid all signs of beauty quite waste. Nor if anyone that had known the place before and had come on it suddenly now, would he have known it again.[41]

When the bar-Kochba revolt ended, the Roman historian Dio Cassius wrote, "All of Judea became almost a desert."[42] God once called Israel "the most beautiful of all lands."[43] Now it stood barren, and His chosen people were scattered to the winds.

> I will lay waste the land, so that your enemies who live there will be appalled. I will scatter you among the nations and will draw out my sword and pursue you. Your land will be laid waste, and your cities will lie in ruins.[44]

This was only the beginning of the covenant curses. The Jews were about to face an even fiercer enemy—one that bore the name "Christian."

8

The Church Grows Teeth

As hard as the Romans were on the Jews, in a sense they were forgiving, too. Their law gave the Jews certain protection and privileges, including Roman citizenship. Except for the time of Hadrian, Judaism was accepted. As long as the Jews were content with Roman rule, the Empire let them alone.

The real trouble for the chosen people started with the Christianization of the Roman Empire. It is a part of the Old Covenant story few people know, and those who do know don't like to talk about it. It is too painful for Jews and too condemning for Christians. This grim part of the story exposes the darkest hours of Church history and, consequently, it has been swept under the rug.

But the story must be told—not hidden. Not only is it crucial to a real understanding of the Bible, it is the key to understanding today's news and being prepared for tomorrow's. It began in A.D. 313 when Constantine converted to Christianity and became the first in a long line of "Christian" emperors. Christianity soon became the favored religion.

And as the Church grew in legal and political power, it soon flexed its new-found muscles against its old nemesis—the Jews. Christians had long been the object of Jewish persecution and scorn; now the Church was in the position to return the action, which it did with a vengeance.

Aware of the Old Covenant and its curses, the Church believed it was the duty of the Christian State to make sure those curses found the Jewish "Christ-killers." The Church appointed itself as God's instrument of vengeance. Beginning with Constantine, Jewish persecution was legal under Roman law. It was considered just punishment for the crucifixion of the Messiah. The Emperor Justinian (527-565) summarized the attitude behind the anti-Jewish laws of "Christian" Rome.

> They [the Jews] shall enjoy no honors. Their status shall reflect the perverse condition which they have desired in their souls.[1]

In other words, "They asked for it, and we are going to give it to them." The new policy of Rome was to make the life of Jews as miserable as possible so they would see the sin they had committed against God and be brought to repentance.

This was incredibly naive. People are no more attracted to Christ by persecution than bees can be lured with vinegar. The Jews were driven farther and farther from their Messiah by the actions of those who carried His name. Although some of these antagonizers were only political Christians because of political and economic advantages, to an outsider it all presented a united Christian "front."

Juris Imprudence

Most of the anti-Semitic laws of Rome were aimed at harassing the Jews and stopping the spread of what Constantine called "their perverse and vicious sect." Under the new laws, a Jew who converted a Christian to Judaism was to be killed and his property confiscated. The same fate awaited any Jew who attacked a Jewish convert to Christianity. Any Christian who voluntarily converted to Judaism was stripped of all money and property.[2]

To further impede the growth of Judaism, a ban was placed on the construction of new synagogues, and only those in danger of falling down could be repaired.[3] Jews were forbidden to marry Christians, also under penalty of death, and many marriages that had already taken place were dissolved.[4]

To make the legal discrimination complete, the Emperor Justinian decreed that no Jewish person could be a credible witness against a Christian in court. If a Christian wronged a Jew, the Jew always lost in court unless he could find a Christian who would support him.[5]

Since it was hopeless to obtain justice, the Jews established their own courts and jails. Some Jewish communities imposed the death penalty on a Jew who informed on another Jew in a Christian court, since he had surely condemned his brother.[6]

The Roman laws even regulated what could be read and taught by Jews in their synagogues. It was forbidden for any public reading of the Old Testament to be followed by an interpretation of the rabbis as found in the Talmud or Mishnah (which were collections of the teaching of ancient rabbis). These books were banned, and permissible interpretations of Old Testament passages were strictly regulated.

It was forbidden to teach or publicly read Bible prophecies dealing with the future restoration and rebuilding of Israel. Such prophecies were interpreted to apply only to the Church. The Biblical doctrine of an Israel-centered Kingdom of God was changed to a Church-centered one. By law, Israel was declared rejected by God. All of her covenant promises were claimed by the Church-State.[7]

Tragically, these early Christian-Roman laws became the model for later European governments. They set the pattern for legal harassment of Jews throughout the Middle Ages. They regulated Jewish social life in many parts of Europe until the 1800s.

> . . .You will be unsuccessful in everything you do; day after day you will be oppressed and robbed, with no one to rescue you.
>
> You will be pledged to be married to a woman, but another will take

her and ravish her. You will build a house, but you will not live in it. . . .Your ox will be slaughtered before your eyes, but you will eat none of it. Your donkey will be forcibly taken from you and will not be returned. . . .

A people that you do not know will eat what your land and labor produce, and you will have nothing but cruel oppression all your days.

The sights you see will drive you mad.[8]

A Tree Cutting Its Own Roots

One of the main concerns of the early Church was to "de-Judaize" itself—to shake off every remnant of the religion of the accursed "Christ-killers." The first Council of Nicea (A.D. 325) decreed that the Church must celebrate the Passover season (Good Friday and Easter) at a time different from the Jews. The date was fixed at the first Friday after the first full moon in spring (the Jewish feast was celebrated two weeks after the first new moon, or in the Jewish calendar, on the 14th of Nisan). Constantine was in charge of the Nicean council.

It is unbecoming beyond all measure that on this, the holiest of festivals, we should follow the customs of the Jews. Henceforward let us have nothing to do with this odious people. Our Savior has shown us another path.

It would indeed be absurd if the Jews were able to boast that we are not in a position to celebrate the Passover without the aid of their rules [calculations].[9]

It was the rabbis in Palestine who knew the astronomy for charting the phases of the moon. Based on the Biblical lunar calendar, they set the times for the Jewish feasts. The Christians had abandoned the "Jewish" calendar. Too proud to ask the rabbis for the real date of Passover, they fixed their own date.[10]

To this day, the Church uses the Nicean formula in determining the Easter season. It is only by accident that we sometimes celebrate Passover on the day God established in Leviticus 23:5.

The Council of Laodicea (343-380) continued "de-Judaizing" itself, forbidding Christians to keep the Jewish Sabbath, the Old Testament feasts, or even to eat matzo—Jewish unleavened bread.[11]

In evidence of our lost Old Testament heritage, many churches celebrate communion with leavened bread (bread with yeast), although Jesus and the apostles probably would have considered this sacrilegious. In the Bible, leaven represents sin. At the Last Supper, which was a Passover meal, Jesus lifted up a piece of unleavened bread to symbolize His sinless (unleavened) body.[12]

God required unleavened bread as a symbol of the sinless state of the believer who has his sins removed by the sacrifice of the Passover lamb. The first Christians recognized Jesus as the true Passover Lamb, "who takes away the sin of the world." They saw tremendous prophetic fulfillment in Him.

> Get rid of the old yeast that you may be a new batch without yeast—as you really are. For Christ, our Passover Lamb, has been sacrificed. Therefore let us keep the Festival, not with the old yeast, the yeast of malice and wickedness, but with bread without yeast, the bread of sincerity and truth.[13]

The Church had separated itself so completely from the Jews that the Old Testament was either ignored as "Jewish" or allegorized beyond recognition. It almost became scandalous to speak of Jesus as Jewish. Some theologians even tried to prove that, because of His miraculous birth, Jesus had no Jewish blood in Him.

The Church learned to despise her Jewish roots, even seeking to cut herself off from her own heritage. Yet this attitude was condemned by the New Testament.

> If some of the branches have been broken off [referring to unbelieving

Jews], and you, though a wild olive shoot, have been grafted in among the others and now share in the nourishing sap from the olive root, do not boast over those branches. If you do, consider this: You do not support the root, but the root supports you.[14]

Fair Game

Yet Jewish people continued to be reviled from Christian pulpits in terms that would ring dollar signs in the eyes of libel lawyers.

Brothel and theater, the synagogue is also a cave of pirates and the lair of wild beasts. . . .Living for their belly, mouth forever gaping, the Jews behave no better than hogs and goats in their lewd grossness and the excess of their gluttony.

Jews are possessed by demons.[15]

This came from the "golden tongue" of St. John Chrysostom, the bishop of Constantinople (344-407). Chrysostom means "golden tongued"—a reference to his celebrated power of preaching.

The Church's characterization of Jewish people as demon-possessed devil worshipers made them very sinister in the minds of Christians. All sorts of incredible tales were concocted. The belief that Jews had tails (like the devil) persisted in Spain until the nineteenth century.[16]

Leon Poliakov, a modern Jewish historian, recorded some of the outrageous beliefs many Christians had about Jews in the Middle Ages.

They are born misshapen, they are hemorrhoidal and man as well as women afflicted with menstruation. . . .

The descendants of [the tribe of] Simeon bleed four days every year, those of Benjamin have worms in their mouth and so on.[17]

Hundreds of years of anti-Semitic propaganda made the

Christians see Jewish people as sub-human. Added to this was the Church's self-appointed role as God's executioner of the Old Testament curses. The Jews became "fair game" wherever they went. They were convenient scapegoats upon whom Christians could vent their anger and frustration.

There is probably not a crime imaginable for which the Jews were not blamed. Christians spread vicious lies, saying that Jewish people used Christian babies as human sacrifices for Passover rites. Many Jews "confessed" under torture rather than face death at the hands of the Church persecutors.[18]

Because the Jews were considered demonic and dangerous, the Church made sure that they were easily identified in society. In 1215 Pope Innocent III and the Fourth Lateran Church Council ordered the Jews to wear distinctive hats and yellow arm badges. They were also segregated into communities apart from Christians. Thus the ghetto was born.[19] But many Jewish people fled to Poland. Still a "pagan" country, Poland welcomed the refugees.[20]

Pope Innocent was merely continuing the same "remedy" for "the Jewish problem" that had been passed down for 800 years.

> The Jews against whom the blood of Jesus Christ cries out, although they ought to be slain lest the Christian people forget the divine law, ought nevertheless to be dispersed over the earth as wanderers, so their countenance might be full of shame and they might seek for the name of the Lord Jesus Christ.[21]

Later popes perpetuated Innocent's edict. Pope Paul IV issued a Papal Bull on July 12, 1555, concerning ghettos.

> In Rome and all the other cities of the Papal States, the Jews shall live entirely separate from the Christians, in a quarter or a street with one entrance and one exit. They shall build no new synagogue nor own real estate.[22]

When the Black Plague of 1348-49 killed one-third of the

European population, the Jews were accused of causing it by poisoning the wells of the Christians. (It is now known that the Plague is caused by rats and is spread by fleas.)

The rat is an unclean animal according to Leviticus 11, so Jews would have been more careful to remove them from their houses and communities than Gentiles. It is possible that because of this, Jews were not hit as hard by the plague; and when Gentiles saw this, they put two and two together and came up with five, thinking the Jews had something to do with the Plague.[23]

This slander so enraged the Gentile population that they formed mobs and wiped out more than 350 Jewish ghettos in Germany alone. An eyewitness reported that tens of thousands of Jewish men, women, and children were "murdered, drowned, burned, broken on the wheel, hanged, exterminated, strangled, buried alive, and tortured to death."[24]

But the nightmare for Jewish people living in Europe did not end. It continued unabated.

The year 1411 was fateful for the Jews of Spain. This year the Spanish Inquisition began. During its reign, terror spread across Spain and the rest of Catholic Europe. For the next 300 years, anyone suspected of being a Jew or a "heretic" was imprisoned and tortured until he recanted or was executed.

Vincent Ferrer, a Dominican friar who was later declared a saint, marched through Castille at the head of a mob of looters and fanatics. He would burst into synagogues on the Sabbath with a Torah scroll in one hand, a crucifix in the other, and offer the assembled Jews a simple choice: baptism or death. Thousands were killed, but Ferrer boasted that he alone had baptized 35,000 Jews.[25]

Thomas de Torquemada, the grand inquisitor, finally decided that the only way to rid Spain of the Jewish heresy was to remove the Jews. He persuaded King Ferdinand and Queen Isabella to sign the edict expelling all Jews from Spain just as they had been expelled from England in 1290 and from France in

1306. Allowed four months to prepare, they could take only their personal effects. Their gold, silver, and jewels were confiscated by the Church and State.[26]

The edict was signed March 31, 1492, the year Columbus set out for the "Indies." Columbus recorded the event in his diary.

> In the same month in which Their Majesties issued the edict that all the Jews should be driven out of the Kingdom and its territories, in the same month they gave me the order to undertake with sufficient men my expedition of discovery to the Indies.[27]

Three centuries later, the French philosopher Montesquieu took a long look back over the three hundred years of the Inquisition. He wrote a scathing commentary on the events of those years.

> If anyone in the days to come should ever dare to say that the people of Europe were civilized in the century in which we are now living, you [the church government] will be cited as proof that they are barbarians.[28]

As if the Spanish Inquisition were not enough, in 1509 fanatical "defenders of the faith" set out on a crusade under a call from Pope Urban II. The purpose of the crusade was to "liberate" the Holy Land from the Moslem "infidels" who had conquered it. The call went out in November and, by the following summer, 200,000 hopeful crusaders had gathered in France for the march to Palestine.

But its leaders found an enemy closer to home. Considered infidels as much as the Moslems, Jewish people also became the crusaders' target for annihilation. The crusaders spread terror across Europe for the Jews. Whole villages were wiped out. Thousands were driven into synagogues, then burned alive. Many Jews chose to take their own lives rather than face the barbarians.[29]

The Protestant Reforms

Even during the Protestant Reformation of the 1500s, when many countries broke away from the Catholic Church, Christians still could not free themselves from their hatred of Jews. Martin Luther gave a sad commentary on the anti-Semitism of Christians.

> If it is a mark of a good Christian to hate the Jews, what excellent Christians all of us are.[30]

Luther is an interesting study in anti-Semitism. After making his famous break with Catholicism, Luther clearly saw the hideousness of the barbaric crimes the Church had committed against God's chosen. Luther powerfully demonstrated the Biblical teachings concerning the Jews: they will eventually return to their rejected Messiah. In his pamphlet, "Jesus Was Born a Jew," Luther launched a tirade against the Church.

> Our imbeciles, the papists and the bishops . . . have treated the Jews as if they were dogs, not men. They have done nothing but persecute them. The Jews are the blood relatives, the cousins and brothers of our Lord and. . .belong to Jesus Christ much more than we do. Hence I beg my dear papists to call me a Jew, when they are tired of calling me a heretic.[31]

Trying to rebuild the long-burned bridges, Luther made many overtures into the Jewish communities in Germany. He found the Jews more than his match. Understandably suspicious of anyone who labeled himself "Christian," they did not welcome him with open arms as he expected.

As time went on and the Jews remained unimpressed (they even converted some of his Protestants), Luther turned against them. Becoming viciously anti-Semitic, he recommended the revival of all the traditional Jewish "cures," including expulsion, confiscation of goods, and synagogue burning.

What then shall we Christians do with this damned, rejected race of Jews? . . . We must prayerfully and reverentially practice a merciful severity. Perhaps we can save a few from the fire and the flames. We must not seek vengeance. They are surely being punished a thousand times more than we might wish them. Let me give you my honest advice.

First, their synagogues or churches should be set on fire, and whatever does not burn up should be covered or spread over with dirt so that no one may be able to see a cinder or stone of it. And this ought to be done for the honor of God and of Christianity in order that God may see that we are Christians, and that we have not wittingly tolerated or approved of such public lying, cursing and blaspheming of His Son and His Christians. . . .

Secondly, their homes should likewise be broken down and destroyed. For they perpetrate the same things there that they do in their synagogues. . . .

Fourthly, their rabbis must be forbidden under threat of death to teach any more.[32]

Luther's anti-Semitic works not only influenced the Germany of his time but, four hundred years later, made a tragic impression on young Adolph Hitler.[33] In *Mein Kampf* he wrote, "Hence today I believe that I am acting in accordance with the will of the Almighty Creator; by defending myself against the Jew, I am fighting for the work of the Lord."

Jews and the New Paganism

The first real sign of hope for the European Jews was the French Revolution of 1789. Like its American counterpart, this revolution was modeled after the ideas of the Humanist philosophers who affirmed the value of every man. The Humanists were mostly Deists who rejected the Biblical ideas of a personal God Who was involved in the affairs of mankind.

Because of this move away from Christianity, the Jews had their first real opportunity to exist as full and equal citizens in a

European country. It was the American colonies that first allowed citizenship rights for Jews.[34]

However, it was not long before the monster of anti-Semitism took on a different form. A new secular hatred soon united with the older religious persecutions. This time the Jew was not only seen as a "Christ-killer," but also as part of an economic conspiracy to take over the world.

For the past thousand years, the Jews had been forced into moneylending because Christians believed it was against Biblical law to accept interest on loans. They did not want to make loans themselves, yet they wanted capital for business reasons. Most of the interest profits the Jews made were taxed by the Church and State. In this way, the government could gain all the benefits of moneylending without actually "dirtying its hands."[35]

But because of this experience in money matters, some Jewish people, like the Rothschilds, started gaining tremendous wealth in banking when the persecutions diminished and they were allowed to keep their profits.[36]

Jews were now found in government posts. Because they shared a common language and culture, they were able to use their business skills and abilities to communicate across national barriers. For this reason, they became valuable assets to their governments.

This new high visibility fueled the conspiracy fires. Soon stories started circulating about the "Elders of Zion," a supposedly secret organization out to take over the world, and every Jew was suspect.

Jews now took on the image of conspiratorial bankers and politicians. They were considered the cause of every economic setback and political turnover. This new non-religious anti-Semitism is strong today. Many still think the Jews are conspiring to control the banks and the various forms of media, such as television, movies, and the news, in the United States and in Europe.

Nevertheless, conspiracy did not place Jews in prominent positions throughout the world. God is keeping them in the public eye. Because of the Old Covenant, Israel cannot help but be on center stage. As God's witnesses, Israel's blessings or curses will always be telegraphed to the world.

Back to Zion

During the European persecutions, the Jews were driven into the more pagan eastern Europe and Russia. Eventually this area, too, came under a Church-State government. For the Jews, the results were sadly predictable—ghettos, persecution, and mass exterminations. In 1727 Catherine I ordered all Jews to leave Russia—an order that was never fully carried out. The Russians quickly realized how much they needed the Jews' business skills for, in the short time they were gone, Russia almost went bankrupt.[37]

In 1861 Czar Alexander II started a reform movement under the slogan, "One Russia, One Creed, One Czar." "One Creed" meant that all Russians were to unite under the Orthodox Church. When Jews resisted this forced conversion, the government started a series of "pogroms" to frighten them into submission. The pogroms were organized terrorist raids on Jewish ghettos.[38]

In 1898 one of the aids to Czar Nicolas II suggested the following mathematically precise solution to Russia's "Jewish problem": exterminate one-third, convert one-third, and drive one-third to emigrate.[39] In addition, the pogroms continued. When news of the pogroms reached a shocked world, a storm of protest was raised similar to that against Soviet Russia's treatment of Jews today.

The pogroms were a bitter awakening for the Jews. Even the new "enlightened" world would not let them alone. Many Jews felt that the only hope for their kind was to return to Palestine and set up their own Jewish state. This idea was first called

Zionism in 1893, after Mt. Zion outside of Jersualem. According to many Biblical prophecies, Israel would be regathered back to her homeland after the covenant curses, and the Messiah would come and reign on Mt. Zion to deliver His people from oppression.[40]

But Zionism was a messianic movement without a messiah. Instead of a person, the messiah of the Zionists was the idea of a Jewish state on Jewish soil. Just as the prophecies pictured the Messiah as the one who would deliver Israel from her enemies, the return to Zion would rescue the Jews from their enemy—the world.

At first Zionism produced mostly hostility from those it was supposed to help. Most Jews felt that it was the Messiah's job to reestablish the state of Israel, and they considered it blasphemy for the Jews to set it up without him.

The Zionist dream remained out of reach. It would take the most barbaric crime of all time to make Zionism a reality.

The Holocaust

. . . You will become a thing of horror to all the kingdoms on earth. . . .

All these curses. . .will be a sign and a wonder to you and your descendants forever. . . .You who were as numerous as the stars in the sky will be left few in number, because you did not obey the Lord your God.[41]

With the crush of Hitler's Third Reich, the world became familiar with such names as Auschwitz, Dachau, and Belsen. Six million Jews had perished.

The word *holocaust* means "burnt offering." For the Jews it was the only appropriate word to describe the annihilation of one-third of their people.

To the Jewish people, the message was clear. No matter how enlightened or advanced the world became, one thing remained constant—hatred of the Jew. The return to Zion became more than an idea. Now it was a necessity, an instinctive drive that would be fought and died for.

After the war, thousands of Jewish refugees fled from Germany, Poland, and Russia. Most countries refused them entrance and for many, their destination became Israel. They came on old tankers and anything else that would float, but when they arrived in Palestine, many were turned back by the British authorities who now controlled that territory.

For the more militant Jews, the British became another Gentile enemy. Fierce guerrilla warfare broke out between the Jews and the British. England decided that keeping Palestine was not worth the trouble, so it agreed to a United Nations' plan to partition Palestine, giving part to the Jews and part to the Arab "Palestinians" living there.

Israel Reborn

Who has ever heard of such a thing?
Who has ever seen such things?

Can a nation be born in a day
or a nation be brought forth in a moment?[42]

On May 14, 1948, British control over Palestine ended, and Israel was reborn after 1,878 years of exile. The next day Israel was attacked by a united army from Egypt, Syria, Lebanon, Iraq, Jordan, Saudi Arabia, and Yemen. Amazingly, Israel won.

Many of the Palestinians, those who had taken up arms against Israel or who were simply caught in the middle, fled to Jordan and Lebanon. They became the famous Palestinian refugees who are now demanding the right to set up their own state in Israel.

Meanwhile, Arabs and Jews continue to fight periodic wars, and world criticism of Israel mounts daily.

The Jews look upon Israel as the "ingathering of the exiles" who were banished from the land almost two thousand years ago. Many Israelis saw 1948 as the year of the fulfillment of the Biblical prophecies that promised the return of Abraham's seed to the Promised Land. This note of prophetic fulfillment is reflected in the Declaration of Independence of the State of Israel.

> It is the natural right of the Jewish people, like any other people, to control their own destiny in their own sovereign state. The State of Israel will be open to Jewish immigration and the ingathering of the exiles. It will devote itself to developing the land for the good of all its inhabitants. It will rest upon the foundations of liberty, justice, and peace as invisioned by the prophets of Israel.

Israel and Armageddon

"Then the nations will know that I am the Lord," declares the Sovereign Lord, "when I show myself holy through you [Israel] before their eyes."[43]

An unbelieving Israel continues to fulfill its Old Covenant role as an involuntary witness to the world. Israel remains front-page news, and a God-rejecting world grows increasingly hostile toward the seed of Abraham. The Bible predicts a time when the whole world will stand against Israel. The last world war will take place over Israel when God "will gather all the nations to Jerusalem to fight against it."[44]

God's original intent to show Himself to a hostile world through Israel has not changed. It is still through Israel that the world will come to know the power and holiness of God. This will happen when the nations are allied against Israel to remove the only obstacle to peace in the oil-rich Middle East. We have already reached the point where the nations can be forced to sell Israel for oil. When the world has once again decided upon the "final solution to the Jewish problem," and their armies are gathered against God's chosen, it will collide with God head-on.

I will gather all the nations to Jerusalem to fight against it. . . .

Then the Lord will go out and fight against those nations, as he fights in the day of battle.[45]

The Church on Trial

And what is the result of the Church's role in Jewish history? In his book *The Anguish of the Jews,* Father Edward H. Flannery relates an incident that graphically portrays the normal reaction of many Jewish people to the cross today.

> One evening several years ago, I walked north on Park Avenue in New York City in the company of a young Jewish couple. Behind us shone the huge illuminated cross the Grand Central Building displays each year at Christmas time. Glancing over her shoulder, the young lady—ordinarily well disposed toward Christianity—declared, "That cross makes me shudder. It is like an evil presence."

> This disturbing comment evoked many questions in me, not the least of which was, "How did the cross, the supreme symbol of universal love, become a sign of fear, of evil for this young Jewess?"[46]

The most shocking aspect of the fulfillment of the Old Covenant is how the Church was so much a part of the curses brought upon the Jews. Throughout their history, Jews have suffered unimaginably at the hands of those who called themselves "Christians." Even Adolph Hitler found justification for his holocaust from sermons like those of Martin Luther, encouraging his followers to burn down synagogues.

How can the actions of the Church be defended? They cannot.

The Church had no business interfering in God's covenant with Israel. If Israel was to fail in the covenant and to communicate to the world through her curses, that was between God and Israel. God did not, and does not, need help. He never gave Christians, or anyone else, the right or the authority to play executioner. In fact He promised that He would curse those who cursed Abraham.

> I will bless those who bless you, and whoever curses you I will curse.[47]

Even more to the point, God promised that those who brought the curses of the Old Covenant upon Israel would likewise be cursed.

> When all these blessings and curses I have set before you come upon you. . .the Lord will put all these curses on your enemies who hate and persecute you.[48]

The curses had to come if Israel was disobedient, but that did not excuse the people who would bring them.

> Woe to the world because of the things that cause people to sin! Such things must come, but woe to the man through whom they come.[49]

With frightening prophetic insight, the prophet Jeremiah foresaw a time when Jews would be persecuted by those who would justify their actions because of Israel's disobedience against God.

> They [Israel] wandered over mountain and hill
>   and forgot their own resting place.
> Whoever found them devoured them;
>   their enemies said, "We are not guilty,
> for they sinned against the Lord, their true pasture,
>   the Lord, the hope of their fathers."[50]

Similarly, Obadiah condemns the Edomites (a nation southeast of Israel) because they gloated over Israel in her day of punishment.

On the day you stood aloof
  while strangers carried off his wealth
and foreigners entered his gates
  and cast lots for Jerusalem,
    you were like one of them.
You should not look down on your brother
  in the day of his misfortune,
nor rejoice over the people of Judah
  in the day of their destruction,
nor boast so much
  in the day of their trouble.
You should not march through the gates of my people
  in the day of their disaster,
nor look down on them in their calamity
  in the day of their disaster,
nor seize their wealth
  in the day of their disaster. . .
As you have done, it will be done to you;
  your deeds will return upon your own head.[51]

This prophecy, originally directed against Edom because of her gloating over the fall of Jerusalem in 586 B.C., fit so well with the Church's persecution of Jews, that the term *Edom* became synonymous with the *Christian Church-State* (Rome) in many Jewish writings, including the Talmud.[52]

The actions of the Church against Israel were inexcusable, and the Church has been paying severely for it. In cursing the seed of Abraham, the Church brought the curse of God upon itself. One doesn't have to be a historian to realize that the Church quickly became perverted after it gained political power and started its policy of anti-Semitism. The Church soon lost any resemblance to its founder. What the Church has perpetrated against the Jewish people has not been because of Jesus, but in spite of everything He ever taught.

In the Book of Revelation, Jesus told disobedient churches that He would "remove your lampstand out of its place."[53] The lamp is symbolic of God's presence. The shining lamp of His presence is how the world can see God working in and through the Church or a believer.[54] If a lampstand is removed from a congregation, it means that God has taken His presence from that church. The world can no longer see God's work in this cursed congregation because of its darkness.

For much of its history the Church has cowered in great darkness. But God is bringing renewal to His Church, and Christians are starting to see the importance of Israel in God's plans.

Many congregations now have outreaches into the Jewish community. Christians are trying to repair the broken bridges. Such organizations as Jews for Jesus and The American Board of Missions to the Jews are breaking down the barriers that have risen over the last two thousand years.

Commendable changes have taken place in the institutional church. In 1976 the Southern Presbyterian Church became the first denomination to include in its Declaration of Faith the statement that the Church has not replaced Israel in God's plans.

> We can never lay exclusive claim to being God's people as though we had replaced those to whom the covenant, the law and the promises belong.
>
> We affirm that God had not rejected His people the Jews. The Lord does not take back His promises.
>
> We Christians have rejected Jews throughout our history with shameful prejudice and cruelty.
>
> God calls on us to dialogue and cooperation that we do not ignore our real disagreement, yet proceed in mutual love and respect.
>
> We are bound together with them in a single story of those chosen to serve and proclaim the living God.[55]

During the Second Vatican Council in 1963, the Catholic Church, for the first time in its history, declared through Pope John XXIII that it does not condemn the Jewish race for the crucifixion of Jesus.

We now acknowledge that for many, many centuries blindness has covered our eyes, so that we no longer see the beauty of Thy chosen people and no longer recognize in its face the features of our first-born brother. We acknowledge that the mark of Cain is on our brow. For centuries Abel lay low in blood and tears because we forgot Thy love. Forgive us the curse that we wrongfully pronounced upon the name of the Jews. Forgive us that we crucified Thee in the flesh for the second time. For we knew not what we did.[56]

Billy Graham made the following assessment of Church history upon receiving the National Interreligious Award from the American Jewish Committee.

The institutional church has sinned through much of its history and has much to answer for at the judgment, especially the anti-Semitism practiced against the Jewish people.[57]

As far as Israel is concerned, it is a miracle that she is still a nation.

. . .let Israel now say, "Many times they have persecuted me from my youth up; yet they have not prevailed against me."[58]

9

The God-Man
Messiah

The world is looking for a man.

We seem to have lost faith in systems and formulas. People are searching instead for the man who has all the answers. An often-repeated quote from a former minister of the European Economic Community illustrates this lust for a leader. "Send us a man who can hold the allegiance of all the people, and whether he be God or devil, we will receive him."[1]

He is right; we do need a man. But we must not be so quick to throw away his moral credentials. Tragically, the world is growing so desperate for a leader that it is willing to overlook his moral aberrations.

Long ago God recognized the need for a special person to rule this rebel planet. From the beginning, He promised the coming of a unique God-Man to govern our world. Israel has known for centuries about this coming King, the Messiah. His title comes from the Hebrew practice of anointing kings with olive oil when they were inaugurated.

The oil symbolized the descent of the Holy Spirit upon the king. At his inauguration, the king became a *Mashiach,* an anointed one. Through the shuffle of languages, *Mashiach* becomes "Messiah" in English, and in Greek the word is *Christos,* which gives us the word "Christ." So the words *Messiah* and *Christ* are synonymous. They all point to the one with the oil (spirit) poured on him.

Since all Israelite kings were anointed, they were all messiahs—the Lord's anointed.[2] But the prophets foretold the coming of a special anointed one who would take control of this world, end the Babylonian rebellion, and establish His throne in Jerusalem, making Israel the chief of the nations.

The prophecies go all the way back to Eden, where God first promised the coming of one who would "bruise" Satan's head (in other words, deliver a fatal blow).[3] Centuries later Moses prepared the people for a prophet "like me" who would lead the nation.[4]

David's Deal

About 1000 B.C. God made a covenant with David, promising that the Messiah would be born in his family. This Davidic Covenant is based on the agreement with Abraham, since it involves Abraham's promised people and land. Therefore, it takes its place as one of the covenants preparing the way for Armageddon and the coming of the Kingdom of God.

David's covenant is like Abraham's in that it was one-sided: it demanded little of David. It also resembles Abraham's foundation covenant in that it doesn't seem important at first glance.

"When your days are over and you go to be with your fathers, I will raise up your offspring to succeed you, one of your own sons, and I will establish his kingdom. He is the one who will build a house for me, and I will establish his throne forever. I will be his father, and he will be my son. I will never take my love away from him, as I took it away from your predecessor [Saul]. I will set him over my house and my kingdom forever; his throne will be established forever."[5]

The Son of God

What is crucial about the Messiah is not so much what He does but who He is. From the beginning, the Messiah was said to be the Son of God. Many other prophecies confirmed this. In

Psalm 2, God says of Him, "You are my son; today I have begotten you."[6]

Isaiah shows the astonishing ramifications of what it means for the Messiah to be the Son of God.

> For to us a child is born, to us a son is given, and the government will be on his shoulders.
>
> And he will be called Wonderful Counselor, Mighty God, Everlasting Father, Prince of Peace.
>
> Of the increase of his government and peace there will be no end.
>
> He will reign on David's throne and over his kingdom, establishing and upholding it with justice and righteousness from that time on and forever.[7]

Because he was the Son of God, the Messiah would be called, "Mighty God," "Everlasting Father," or "Father of Eternity." These are titles only God can rightly claim.

Today it is no big deal to think of someone being a son of God. We are used to thinking of ourselves as sons of God because we are adopted into His family. But to be the "only begotten son of God"—as the Messiah was said to be—is something unique. The secret to the Messiah's identity is wrapped up in the terms *begotten* and *created*. C. S. Lewis, in his book *Mere Christianity,* explains these words in simple language.

> We don't use the words *begetting* or *begotten* much in modern English, but everyone still knows what they mean. To beget is to become the father of: to create is to make. And the difference is this. When you beget, you beget something of the same kind as yourself. A man begets human babies, a beaver begets little beavers and a bird begets eggs which turn into little birds. But when you make, you make something of a different kind from yourself. A bird makes a nest, a beaver builds a dam, a man makes a wireless set—or he may make something more like himself than a wireless set: say a statue. If he is a clever enough carver he may make a statue which is very like a man indeed. But, of course, it is not a real man; it only looks like one. It cannot breathe or think. It is not alive.

Now that is the first thing to get clear. What God begets is God; just
as what man begets is man. What God creates is not God; just as
what man makes is not man. That is why men are not sons of God in
the sense that Christ is.[8]

The Jews knew that it was special to be called the Son of God.
It was a title of deity, applied only to the Messiah. They thought of
the Messiah as more like God than a man. They were looking for
a Divine Messiah who would be worshiped even by the angels.[9]
In fact the nature of the expected Messiah was so close to that of
Jehovah Himself, that at times the Messiah and Jehovah God
are presented as one.[10]

The popular concept of the Divine Messiah was greatly
influenced by God's warning to Moses that no one could look at
Him in His glory and live.[11] So the people expected a Messiah
who would come riding on the clouds in radiant glory to take control of Earth.

Accordingly, it was considered blasphemy for a mere mortal
to claim to be the Messianic "Son of God." This blasphemy was
punishable by death under the Old Covenant Law.[12]

And this is where things got sticky for Jesus. He was the
Messiah, born into the lineage of David and begotten by the Holy
Spirit. So all Jesus had to do was claim to be what He was and
that was enough to spell His doom.

For this reason the Jews tried all the harder to kill him; not only
was he breaking the Sabbath, but he was even calling God his own
Father, making himself equal with God.[13]

The people's logic is revealing. For Jesus to call God His
Father was also to claim equality with God, since God gives birth
to God.

At Jesus' trial before Pilate, when the Roman could not find
any excuse to condemn Him, the Jews appealed to the Jewish
law against blasphemy.

The Jews insisted, "We have a law, and according to that law he must die, because he claimed to be the Son of God."[14]

Notice they did not say, "He claimed to be God," but "He claimed to be the Son of God," which adds up to the same thing. God's begotten Son must also be God. Like begets like.

After His resurrection, Jesus appeared to His apostles and gave special attention to a doubtful Thomas.

> Then he said to Thomas, "Put your finger here; see my hands. Reach out your hand and put it into my side. Stop doubting and believe."
>
> Thomas said to him, "My Lord and My God!"
>
> Then Jesus told him, "Because you have seen me, you have believed; blessed are those who have not seen and yet have believed."[15]

When we compare Jesus' reaction to receiving worship to that of an angel being likewise adored, the lesson becomes blazingly clear.

> I, John, am the one who heard and saw these things. And when I had heard and seen them, I fell down to worship at the feet of the angel who had been showing them to me. But he said to me, "Do not do it! I am a fellow servant with you and with your brothers the prophets and of all who keep the words of this book. Worship God!"[16]

Because the Messiah is the begotten Son of God, He stands above even the angels, receiving their worship.

> And again, when God brings his firstborn into the world, he says, "Let all God's angels worship him."[17]

At the first Church council, held in Nicea in A.D. 389, the Church fathers wanted to define exactly who and what Jesus was. They arrived at a formula which is accurate and Biblical.

They said Jesus was "God from God, light from light, true God from true God; *begotten and not made;* of one substance with the Father, by whom all things were made."[18] (Emphasis added.)

The crucial difference between Jesus and us is that we were created but Jesus was begotten. This makes us less than God, but Jesus is "God from God." He is of a different order than we, and He stands above us.

> He [Jesus] is the image of the invisible God, the *firstborn* over all creation.[19] (Emphasis added.)

The Bible is careful to separate Jesus from the rest of creation. He was begotten, we were created, and that makes all the difference.

A family pet will give the same respect, or disrespect if it is a cat, to all members of the family because it knows that humans are a different kind of being. So it is with us and Jesus. He expects and deserves the same respect and worship as the Father because both are God. Jesus never refused to be worshiped, an act that would be blasphemous if He were not truly God. Jesus Himself said, "You shall worship the Lord your God and serve Him only."[20]

Can Two Be One?

Problems arise when God begets God. It would seem that there are now two Gods, yet as Jesus taught He quoted Deuteronomy 6:8: "Hear, O Israel, the Lord our God, the Lord is one."[21] Here we are about to enter one of the deepest mysteries.

In the physical realm that is our home, when one human begets another, we end up with two separate beings. This is not the case in the spiritual realm. Jesus said, "I and the Father are one," and He was not speaking of a unity in purpose or ideas. The Jews understood His message clearly.

"I and the Father are one."

Again the Jews picked up stones to stone him, but Jesus said to them, "I have shown you many great miracles from the Father. For which of them do you stone me?"

"We are not stoning you for any of these," replied the Jews, "but for blasphemy, because you, a mere man, claim to be God."[22]

Even though it is hard to understand how two persons can be part of the same being, we have been given an illustration to understand what the Godhead is like. The illustration is marriage. When God formed Eve from part of Adam and then brought her to him, Adam immediately saw the symbol of unity that God intended.

The man said, "This is now bone of my bones and flesh of my flesh; she shall be called woman [*ishah*], for she was taken out of man [*ish*].

For this reason a man will leave his father and mother and be united to his wife, and they will become one flesh."[23]

Marriage illustrates how two separate persons can be joined into one. Of course, in the physical realm a total joining is impossible. But marriage—especially sexual intercourse in marriage (becoming "one flesh")—is the example we have been given to understand how two can be one in the spiritual realm.[24]

In God's mathematics, sometimes one plus one equals one.

The best explanation of the problem comes again from the pen of C.S. Lewis.

The human level is a simple and rather empty level. On the human level one person is one being, and any two persons are two separate beings—just as, in two dimensions (say on a flat sheet of paper) one square is one figure, and any two squares are two separate figures. On the divine level you still find personalities; but up there you find them combined in new ways which we, who do not live on that level, cannot imagine. In God's dimension, so to speak, you find a being who is three Persons while remaining one cube. Of course we cannot fully conceive of a Being like that: just as, if we were so made that we perceived only two dimensions in space we could never properly imagine a cube. But we can get a sort of faint notion of it. And when we do, we are then, for the first time in our lives, getting some positive idea, however faint, of something super-personal—something more than a person. It is something we could never have guessed, and yet, once we have been told, one almost feels one ought to have been able to guess it because it fits in so well with all the things we know already.[25]

The Prophecies

Looking forward to the Messiah, many prophets told of His birth, life, ministry, death, resurrection, and spectacular coming in the clouds to set up the Kingdom of God. The prophecies were incredibly specific. They predicted that the Messiah would

—be born in Bethlehem (Micah 5:2), through parents of the tribe of David (1 Chronicles 17:11-14).
—be miraculously born through a virgin mother (Isaiah 7:14).[26]
—be killed (Psalm 22; Daniel 9:26; Zechariah 13:6,7) and die for the sins of the people (Isaiah 53).
—rise from the grave (Psalm 16:8-10).
—return to a repentant Israel when they realized their mistake in killing him (Zechariah 12:10).
—come in power and glory as the King of the Earth (Zechariah 14; Daniel 7:13,14).

These precisioned prophecies were given hundreds of years before Jesus ever walked the Earth. For example, Psalm 22 seems to describe clearly a man being crucified even though it was written about 1000 B.C. Crucifixion would not even be invented for another 500 years![27]

> Dogs have surrounded me; a band of evil men has encircled me,
> they have pierced my hands and my feet. I can count all my bones;
> people stare and gloat over me. They divide my garments among
> them and cast lots for my clothing.[28]

The New Testament accounts of Jesus' crucifixion are detailed and specific that Jesus' hands and feet were pierced and the soldiers cast lots for His garments.[29]

Even more amazing, Daniel predicted that the Messiah would arrive in what we call the first century A.D. Daniel saw that the Messiah would die shortly before the destruction of Jerusalem.

> After the sixty-two "sevens" [groups of seven years], the Anointed
> One will be cut off [killed] and have nothing. The people of the ruler
> who will come will destroy the city and the sanctuary. The end
> will come like a flood.[30]

The Talmud admits that this prophecy works out to the first century A.D. when Jerusalem was destroyed in A.D. 69. But hundreds of years of Christian persecution have trained the Jewish people not to believe that the "Anointed One" who came at the same time was Jesus. Many Jews believe that the Anointed One prophesied in Daniel was not the Messiah, but simply some local leader.[31]

Prophecies like Daniel's became such a sticky issue in the Jewish-Christian debate about the Messiah that many rabbis declared these prophecies "hands off."

> May the bones of those who calculate the [messianic] end be blown
> away![32]

A Job Half-Done

One of the biggest problems concerning the messiahship of Jesus is His half-done mission. For centuries many Jews have rejected the idea of Jesus as Messiah largely because He did not do everything that the prophecies said the Messiah would do. The prophets were crystal clear that the Messiah would set up the Kingdom of God, eliminate war and injustice, and bring renewal to our sad planet. But obviously, things have gone on as usual since Jesus died almost two thousand years ago.

Jesus knew about all the messianic prophecies, and He always claimed to be the one who would set up the Kingdom. But the Messiah's job was complex. It involved much more than the spectacular coming on the clouds and the climactic battle of Armageddon. His mission also was to do away with sin and evil so that the Kingdom could come.

Just looking at the scope of the many messianic promises, one can see that it would be very difficult for one man to fulfill them all at once. How could the Messiah be born, live, die for sins, be raised from the grave, come on the clouds in power and glory, and set up the Kingdom all at the same time? The Jews' inability to accept Jesus as Messiah did not come from their ignorance of the prophecies. They just could not accept that the Messiah would have to come twice—once to die for sins and be raised, and once to set up the Kingdom.

Paradoxically, the ancient rabbis also saw the difficulty of one man fulfilling all the messianic prophecies. Many solved the problem by teaching that there would be two Messiahs. The Talmud teaches the first Messiah would come from the tribe of Joseph. He would be born in Bethlehem, live a natural life, and die for the sins of Israel. Then the Messiah, the son of David, would arrive, riding on the clouds, to set up the Kingdom.[33]

Many rabbis taught that not all the prophecies would be fulfilled. Those which would be brought about depended upon the faithfulness of the people. If they were not worthy, the Messiah would come in the appearance of a poor man riding a donkey.[34] He would be an "earthly" Messiah. But if Israel was worthy, the Messiah would come riding the clouds to set up the Kingdom.

> If they will be righteous, [the Messiah will come] on the clouds of heaven; if they will not be righteous, [he will come] as a poor man riding upon an ass.[35]

Jesus said that He would do it all, but not all at once. He constantly tried to convince His apostles that the prophecies could not happen simultaneously. When the twelve asked about Elijah, whom the prophet Malachi said would reappear before the Messiah's coming, Jesus asked them a stimulating question about the order of prophesied events.

> Jesus replied, "To be sure, Elijah does come first, and restores all things. Why then is it written that the Son of Man must suffer much and be rejected?"[36]

The title "Son of Man" comes from Daniel's prophecies where he saw the glorious coming of the King.

> In my vision at night I looked, and there before me was one like a son of man [a human being], coming with the clouds of heaven. He approached the Ancient of Days [the Father] and was led into his presence. He was given authority, glory and sovereign power; all peoples, nations and men of every language worshiped him. His dominion is an everlasting dominion that will not pass away, and his kingdom is one that will never be destroyed.[37]

At His trial before the chief priests, Jesus was grilled about His claim to be the "Son of Man," the Messiah of Daniel's prophecy.

> The high priest said to him, "I charge you under oath by the living God: Tell us if you are the Christ [the Messiah], the Son of God."

> "Yes, it is as you say," Jesus replied. "But I say to all of you: In the future you will see the Son of Man sitting at the right hand of the Mighty One and coming on the clouds of heaven."

> Then the high priest tore his clothes and said, "He has spoken

blasphemy! Why do we need any more witnesses? Look, now you have heard the blasphemy. What do you think?"

"He is worthy of death," they answered.[38]

Jesus said He would do everything the Messiah was to do, but not in the time the people expected. His glorious coming was still in the future.

The God-Man

The attitude of the high priest introduces our final difficulty. He clearly and accurately combined the terms *Christ* and *Son of God*, so that anyone who claimed to be the Messiah was claiming deity because the Messiah also was the Son of God and therefore equal with God. All Jesus had to do was to claim to be the Messiah and that was considered blasphemy, for He was a man claiming to be God.

The messianic title that Jesus most often applied to Himself was "Son of Man." He did this to draw the minds of the people back to Daniel 7 so they could see that the Messiah was truly divine but also—as Daniel saw Him—a "son of man," a human being.

But how can a man also be God? In one sense the question is completely beyond the scope of our understanding. Yet in another sense, it can be explained to children. Jesus' Father was God. His mother was human. Before Jesus' birth, the angel Gabriel appeared to Mary, telling her what was about to take place. Notice how the angel promises that Jesus will indeed bring in the Kingdom and fulfill all the prophecies. He also gives a simple explanation of the God-Man (all the prophecies alluded to are cited in brackets).

In the sixth month, God sent the angel Gabriel to Nazareth, a town in Galilee, to a virgin [Isaiah 7:14] pledged to be married to a man named Joseph, a descendant of David [I Chronicles 17]. The virgin's name was Mary. The angel went to her and said, "Greetings, you who are highly favored! The Lord is with you."

Mary was greatly troubled at his words and wondered what kind of greeting this might be. But the angel said to her, "Do not be afraid, Mary, you have found favor with God. You will be with child and give birth to a son, and you are to give him the name Jesus ['God Saves']. He will be great and will be called the Son of the Most High [Psalm 2]. The Lord God will give him the throne of his father David, and he will reign over the house of Jacob forever [I Chronicles 17]; his kingdom will never end [Daniel 7]."

"How will this be," Mary asked the angel, "since I am a virgin?"

The angel answered, "The Holy Spirit will come upon you, and the power of the Most High will over-shadow you. So the holy one to be born will be called the Son of God. . . .For nothing is impossible with God."[39]

The time of Jesus' coming to establish the Kingdom largely depends upon Israel. Jesus said to Israel, "You shall not see me again until you say, 'Blessed is he who comes in the name of the Lord.' "[40] The time of the Messiah's return is joined with Israel's acceptance of Jesus. The prophet Zechariah saw that.

They will look upon me, the one they have pierced, and mourn for him as one mourns for an only child, and grieve bitterly for him as one grieves for a firstborn son.[41]

Along with the rest of the world, Israel will receive her Messiah, but not until she realizes who He is. Israel is the key to His coming. That is our hope, but also our worry. How can the seed of Abraham ever be brought to faith in Jesus when His name has meant nothing but pain and suffering?

This is the miracle of the New Covenant.

10
Life to Dry Bones

Few nations are as opposed to Christianity as Israel. Thousands of years of persecution have left many Jews bitter against those who follow Jesus.

Israel recently passed a law imposing stiff prison sentences against certain forms of Christian missionary activity in Israel.[1] In mathematics, many Israelis use a "T" instead of a plus (+) because the latter looks too much like the symbol of persecution and pain—a Christian cross.[2]

Under the Israeli "Law of Return," anyone who can prove Jewish descent from his mother's side of the family and has not forsaken Judaism is automatically considered an Israeli citizen, should he choose to return to the Promised Land. But there is an exception to this rule. It does not apply to Jews who believe that Jesus is the Messiah. Recently this law was challenged by an American woman desiring to return to Israel. Her Jewish heritage was unquestioned, but the Israeli Supreme Court ruled that anyone who believed in Jesus was no longer Jewish. She had denied her culture.[3] Israel is often more tolerant of Jewish atheists, Buddhists, Hindus, and Moslems than to Jews who believe that Jesus is the fulfillment of Judaism.

It is hard to believe that under such hatred, even a few Jews would see past the years of torment and recognize their own Messiah. It is almost ludicrous to think of Israel as a Christian nation, but that's exactly what will happen. The prophecies are clear. Obviously some spectacular change must come.

The New Covenant is a spectacular covenant. It is the climax of all the contracts drawing our world into cataclysmic changes and a golden future. The interaction of the four covenants—the Abrahamic, Old, Davidic, and New—can best be compared to a pebble dropped into a still pond, making a splash with three ripples emanating from it. The splash at the center is Abraham's Covenant. The ring closest to the splash is the Old Covenant, the second is David's, and the third is the New Covenant. Just as the last ripple contains within it all the other waves, so the New Covenant brings all the other covenants into completion. It is God's crowning touch over His Babylonian rehabilitation program. All the covenants are based on Abraham's Covenant, since without the original splash none of the ripples would exist.

By the time the new contract is fulfilled, Israel will know her Messiah and be the center of His Kingdom. All the covenant promises, stretching back to Abraham, will transform our world politically, economically, sociologically, and ecologically. War, poverty, disease, even fear of animals, will no longer exist.

Even better, this covenant changes people—from the inside out. God will turn Babylonian rebels into obedient children, pour His Holy Spirit on them, and forgive their sins.

But the New Covenant is not just for the future. It is available today, as it has been for the last two thousand years.

Starting Over

The only reason the New Covenant is called "New" is because it replaces the Old Sinai agreement that has determined Israel's history for the past 3,500 years. One can really only understand the New Covenant by seeing Israel's failure under the Old.

The Old Covenant curse left Israel scattered throughout the

world. But failure was not the last word for Israel. Even as far back as when Israel made the Old Covenant, God foresaw their failure and prophesied a new way of dealing with the nation.

> When all these blessings and curses I have set before you come upon you and you take them to heart wherever the Lord your God disperses you among the nations, . . . then the Lord your God will restore your fortunes and have compassion on you and gather you again from all the nations where he scattered you . . . He will bring you to the land that belonged to your fathers and you will take possession of it. . . . The Lord your God will circumcise your hearts and the hearts of your descendants, so that you may love him with all your heart and all your soul, and live.[4]

This prophecy, first given to Moses, was repeated many times by many prophets during Israel's history. Always the prophesied pattern of events is the same: Israel starts out in dispersion and failure under the Old Covenant. Then the New Covenant takes over and three things happen.[5]

—Israel is regathered from the nations.

—The people are spiritually changed to recognize God.

—The Kingdom of God comes.

In the Old Covenant, Israel became God's witness to the world. In the New, Israel continues that role, but in a more successful way.

> I will show the holiness of my great name, which has been profaned among the nations, the name you [Israel] have profaned among them. Then the nations will know that I am the Lord, declares the Sovereign Lord, when I show myself holy through you before their eyes.
>
> For I will take you out of the nations; I will gather you from all the countries and bring you back into your own land. I will sprinkle clean water on you, and you will be clean; I will cleanse you from all

your impurities and from all your idols. I will give you a new heart and put a new spirit in you; I will remove from you your heart of stone and give you a heart of flesh. And I will put my Spirit in you and move you to follow my decrees and be careful to keep my laws. You will live in the land I gave your forefathers; you will be my people, and I will be your God.[6]

God wants to show the world a miracle, a miracle so big that everyone will know that God is really there and that He cares about human affairs. The miracle is Israel. God is working through a scattered nation—deeply set in bitterness, failure, and rebellion—to show Himself to the world.

The Regathering

Few people have ever undergone the shattering experience of being evicted from their land and scattered as wanderers among foreign nations. Going through this experience once would be bad enough, but Israel has suffered this twice. The nation was taken to Babylon in 586 B.C. Then 600 years later, Rome banished Israel from the Promised Land. But both times, she was eventually rescued from certain extinction and returned to Abraham's inheritance.

In that day the Lord will reach out his hand a second time to reclaim the remnant that is left of his people from Assyria, from Lower Egypt, from Upper Egypt, from Cush, from Elam, from Babylonia, from Hamath and from the islands of the sea [i.e. the rest of the world].[7]

The most exciting thing about Israel's modern regathering is that it shows we are in the last days.

The Lord will scatter you among the peoples, and only a few of you will survive among the nations to which the Lord will drive you. . . .But if from there you seek the Lord your God, you will find him if you look for him with all your heart and with all your soul.

When you are in distress and all these things have happened to you, then in later days [lit. "end of days"] you will return to the Lord your God and obey him. For the Lord your God is a merciful God; he will not abandon or destroy you or forget the covenant with your forefathers which he confirmed to them by oath.[8]

If Israel is still God's witness and their regathering was prophesied and prepared, why aren't the Jews believers today? All this is in keeping with God's blueprint. It is only after the nation is returned that God sends illumination and revival upon the people. Israel is experiencing the first step of the New Covenant. She is being regathered in unbelief. It is the second stage that will bring Israel to faith.

Dry Bones

The prophet Ezekiel saw the regathering of Israel in a strange vision of dry bones. The bones represented Israel, dispersed throughout the world and as good as dead. But God told Ezekiel to prophesy over the bones and command them back to life. Suddenly bone joined bone, then flesh completed the bodies. Symbolically Ezekiel was seeing Israel regathered from the nations and put back together in the Promised Land.

So I prophesied as I was commanded. And as I was prophesying, there was a noise, a rattling sound, and the bones came together, bone to bone. I looked, and tendons and flesh appeared on them and skin covered them, but there was no breath in them.

Then he said to me, "Prophesy to the breath; prophesy, son of man, and say to it, 'This is what the Sovereign Lord says: Come from the four winds, O breath, and breathe into these slain, that they may live.' " So I prophesied as he commanded me, and breath entered them; they came to life and stood up on their feet—a vast army.[9]

Significantly, Ezekiel saw the regathering happen in two stages. First the bodies came together, but there was no "breath" in them. They were lifeless. It was only after Ezekiel had prophesied a second time that life came into the bodies. In the Hebrew, there is a word play going on here. The words for "breath" and "spirit" are identical. The bodies without "breath" signified Israel without the "spirit." In other words, Israel had been regathered, but not spiritually renewed. The first stage in the New Covenant, Israel's regathering, is clearly separate from the second, her spiritual rebirth.

Water and Spirit

Jeremiah, the prophet who named the New Covenant, detailed the amazing spiritual rebirth that comes with the second stage of the contract.

> "The time is coming," declares the Lord, "when I will make a new covenant with the house of Israel and with the house of Judah. It will not be like the covenant I made with their forefathers when I took them by the hand to lead them out of Egypt, because they broke my covenant though I was a husband to them," declares the Lord.

> "This is the covenant I will make with the house of Israel after that time," declares the Lord. "I will put my law in their minds and write it on their hearts. I will be their God and they will be my people.

> "No longer will a man teach his neighbor, or a man his brother, saying, 'Know the Lord,' because they will all know me, from the least of them to the greatest," declares the Lord.

> "For I will forgive their wickedness and will remember their sins no more."[10]

The biggest reason for Israel's failure under the Old Covenant was that the covenant law was not a part of them. It was written on the stone tablets that Moses brought down from Sinai. The law was external, not internal; one could take it or leave it.

Similarly, today the speed limit law is not written on our minds, only on paper. If we were born with the 55-mile speed limit stamped indelibly on our brains, we would never break the law; it would be natural for us to obey.

The same analogy is true for God's Law. In the Old Covenant, the Law was written on stone. Obedience was voluntary and optional. But in the New Covenant, the Law is "written on the heart." It becomes an integral part of Israel. Now obedience becomes natural, not forced. Ezekiel said that God would "move you to follow my decrees and be careful to follow my laws." What was once external now becomes internal.

Along with this change comes an innate awareness and knowledge of God and the forgiveness of sins. Deuteronomy called this change a "circumcision of heart." Ezekiel described this cleansing from sin and inner change in terms of "water" and "Spirit."

> I will sprinkle clean water on you, and you will be clean; I will cleanse you from all your impurities. . . . I will give you a new heart and put a new spirit in you. . . . And I will put my Spirit in you and move you to follow my decrees. . . .[11]

This is a staggering change. When the Holy Spirit comes into a person, he is completely changed. Like spiritual Drano, the Holy Spirit goes in and cleans everything out but He never hurts the "pipes." The Spirit gives us a new awareness of God and a new inward motivation. And along with everything else, there is a blanket forgiveness of all sin: immediate salvation.

The change is so radical, Jesus called it being "born again." This severely overused term was coined by Jesus in a conversation with a rabbi about the coming of the Kingdom. Rabbi Nicodemus saw in Jesus the possibility of the Messiah, and he knew that where the Messiah was, the Kingdom could not be far behind. So he came to Jesus to ask about it.

> He [Nicodemus] came to Jesus at night and said, "Rabbi, we know

> that you are a teacher who has come from God. For no one could perform the miraculous signs you are doing if God were not with him."
>
> In reply Jesus declared, "I tell you the truth, unless a man is born again, he cannot see the kingdom of God."
>
> "How can a man be born when he is old?" Nicodemus asked. "Surely he cannot enter a second time into his mother's womb to be born!"[12]

Obviously Nicodemus had missed the whole point. Since "born again" did not communicate, Jesus appealed to his Old Testament learning and rephrased the answer, using the terms "water" and "Spirit" as Ezekiel had done five hundred years before.

> Jesus answered, "I tell you the truth, unless a man is born of water and the Spirit, he cannot enter the kingdom of God. Flesh gives birth to flesh, but the Spirit gives birth to spirit. You should not be surprised at my saying, 'You must be born again.' The wind blows where it pleases. You hear its sound, but you cannot tell where it comes from or where it is going. So it is with everyone born of the Spirit."
>
> "How can this be?" Nicodemus asked.
>
> "You are Israel's teacher," said Jesus, "and do you not understand these things?"

Jesus was surprised that an educated Jew like Nicodemus had overlooked or misunderstood the many Old Testament references to Israel's spiritual change—a change that had to take place before the coming of the Kingdom. Here Jesus was only repeating what the prophets had been saying for centuries. Ezekiel spoke of water, cleansing or forgiveness, and the Spirit; Jeremiah told how someone taking part in the covenant would be inwardly motivated—in effect, march to a different drummer. Jesus simply was saying that Israel had to be spiritually reborn before the Kingdom could come. Step two of the Covenant comes before step three, the Kingdom.

Like the other religious leaders, Nicodemus felt that the prophecies concerning the regathering of Israel (step one) and the religious awakening (step two) had already happened in the Babylonian captivity and return when Israel was cleansed from idolatry. All that Israel now needed for the Kingdom to come was the arrival of the Messiah.

Jesus told him, in effect, that he had left out step two of the New Covenant. Israel still needed to be spiritually awakened, and Jesus was there to bring that renewal.

> Just as Moses lifted up the snake in the desert, so the Son of Man must be lifted up, that everyone who believes in him may have eternal life.
>
> For God so loved the world that he gave his only begotten Son, that whoever believes in him shall not perish but have eternal life.[14]

Here Jesus is referring to Israel's run-in with some very nasty snakes while they were out in the desert after their rescue from Egypt. When the people ran out of food, God provided it from heaven in the form of manna. (*Manna* means "What's that?" It got its name when the Israelites woke up one day and found white stuff all over the ground. They looked down and asked, "Man hu?" and the name stuck.[15])

Gradually, the wondrous surprise at receiving food from Heaven gave way to boredom. Instead of "What's that," they started calling it "miserable food."[16] At this point God was fed up with their insolence and sent them to a place infested with deadly snakes. So many were being bitten that they begged Moses to ask God for help. In response to Moses, God gave the people an unusual snakebite remedy.

> The Lord said to Moses, "Make a snake and put it up on a pole;

anyone who is bitten can look at it and live." So Moses made a bronze snake and put it up on a pole. Then when anyone was bitten by a snake and looked at the bronze snake, he lived.[17]

Obviously this is an unorthodox way to cure snakebite. But God's purpose was prophetic, symbolic of the Messiah. Israel was healed of lethal snakebites by looking at a snake on a pole. Jesus said He would likewise be lifted up on a cross to provide the healing for spiritual snakebite: sin.

The Sacrifice

All covenants were ratified by a sacrifice. God walked between the animal parts for Abraham; the Old Covenant was likewise sealed in blood. But the New Covenant is a special agreement, and a special sacrifice was necessary to put it into effect. At the Last Supper, Jesus took bread and wine and made them into an analogy of His death.

While they were eating, Jesus took bread, gave thanks and broke it, and gave it to his disciples, saying, "Take and eat; this is my body."

Then he took the cup, gave thanks and offered it to them, saying, "Drink from it, all of you. This is my blood of the [new] *covenant,* which is poured out for many for the forgiveness of sins."[18] (Emphasis added.)

It was the sacrifice of the Messiah Himself that put the New Covenant into operation.

As we have seen, one has to enter the confirming sacrifice to take part in a covenant. But sometimes a covenant and its sacrifice are one-sided, like Abraham's contract. All Abraham needed to do was put his trust in the one making the covenant for him, and he would enjoy all the benefits of that contract. When God took Abraham outside to count the stars, giving him an idea of how many offspring he would have, "Abram believed God and it was credited to him as righteousness."[19] All that was demanded of Abraham was trust in God.

This pattern of faith is the same in the New Covenant. The sacrifice was one-sided; the Messiah died alone. And the way to enter the new contract is to believe in the sacrifice and what it promises. Jesus, the Messiah, died as the sacrifice to start the New Covenant. When a person asks to be included in the New Covenant sacrifice, all its spiritual benefits are his, including forgiveness of sins.

But What About the *Goyim*?

Throughout this book, the covenant plan has been viewed from the standpoint of the Jews. The obvious question for *Goyim* (Gentiles) is, "What about me?" For centuries rabbis have debated the question, "Can a Gentile be saved?" Many decided salvation for Gentiles was impossible because the covenants were not given to them. In a way, they were right, for a Gentile must become a spiritual Jew to be saved.

Jesus said, "Salvation is from the Jews."[20] The only way Gentiles can be saved is to be plugged into the Jewish covenant program and become heirs of Abraham. God has provided a simple way for Gentiles to be adopted into Abraham's family and enjoy the covenant blessings of forgiveness and salvation. God's covenants are aimed at winning everyone, not just Israel, back to Himself. He is working through Israel to redeem us all. He has not limited His plans to one nation.

The Bible says that those who believe in the covenant promises like Abraham did are considered Abraham's children, and therefore his heirs, whether they are Jews or Gentiles.

Consider Abraham: "He believed God, and it was credited to him as righteousness." Understand, then, that those who believe are children of Abraham. The Scripture foresaw that God would justify [pronounce innocent] the Gentiles by faith, and announced the

gospel in advance to Abraham: "All nations will be blessed through
you." So those who have faith are blessed along with Abraham, the
man of faith. . . .

You are all sons of God through faith in Christ Jesus, for all of you
who were baptized into Christ [i.e., joined to Him] have been
clothed with Christ. There is neither Jew nor Greek, slave nor free,
male nor female, for you are all one in Christ Jesus. If you belong to
Christ, then you are Abraham's seed, and heirs according to the
promise.[21]

Jesus is the key to joining the covenant program. As the
Messiah, He was the one to whom all the promises ultimately
looked forward. He also was a physical descendant of Abraham.
When someone makes the deal between God and himself to take
part in Jesus' sacrifice, he becomes a part of Christ. He is joined
to Him, or "clothed" with the Messiah. Many times the New
Testament speaks of believers as being "in Christ."[22] We actually become a part of Him; so whatever is His, becomes ours.
Because Jesus is the heir of Abraham, when we are joined to
Him we also become heirs. Nationality does not matter. All
become one in Jesus.

Covenants Old and New

A problem that has bothered the Church for centuries is the
relationship of the Old Covenant to the New, especially that of a
New Covenant believer, a Christian, to the laws and regulations
of the Old Testament. The ancient rabbis counted 613 laws in
the Old Covenant, governing everything from diet and health to
animal sacrifices for the "covering" or "atoning" of sins. This
question would have tremendous consequences on a Christian's
life-style if we should be keeping all 613 rules today. Many of us
have trouble just remembering our phone numbers!

First of all, the Bible is clear that the Old Covenant has been
replaced by the New.

By calling this covenant "new," he [God] has made the first one [the Old Covenant] obsolete; and what is obsolete and aging will soon disappear.[23]

In his letters to the Galatians and the Romans, Paul carefully detailed how the Old Covenant and its laws give way to New Covenant freedom.

In one sense, the Law seems unnecessary. If salvation were free—a gift as far back as Abraham—why were the rules given? First, Paul makes it clear that God did not change rules in the middle of the game by offering free salvation to some while expecting others to earn it. The Law never changed the pattern of Abraham's free salvation.

Brothers, let me take an example from everyday life. Just as no one can set aside or add to a human covenant that has been duly established, so it is in this case. The promises were spoken to Abraham and . . . the law, introduced 430 years later, does not set aside the covenant previously established by God and thus do away with the promise [to Abraham]. For if the inheritance depends on the law, then it no longer depends on a promise; but God in his grace gave it to Abraham through a promise.[24]

The Law and free salvation do not conflict.

Is the law, therefore, opposed to the promises of God? Absolutely not! For if a law had been given that could impart life, then righteousness would certainly have come by the law.

. . .for if righteousness could be gained through the law, Christ died for nothing.[25]

The Law was around for about 1,400 years before Jesus, so if God had wanted to save us by rules and regulations, Jesus had no reason to die. His death would not have changed anything.

Scripture is clear that salvation can never be earned by the Law. Why then was the Law given?

The Law was like a moral babysitter to the human race. It

was given, because of man's spiritual obtuseness, to keep order and morals until the Messiah showed up. The Law was a combination of schoolteacher and policeman. It showed what sin was and demonstrated our moral bankruptcy before God.

> What, then, was the purpose of the law? It was added because of transgressions [sins] until the Seed to whom the promises referred had come.[26]

The Law made us prisoners in that it showed the problem but offered no solutions.

> Now we know that whatever the law says, it says to those who are under the law, so that every mouth may be silenced and the whole world held accountable to God. Therefore no one will be declared righteous in his sight by observing the law; rather, through the law we become conscious of sin.[27]

The "thou shalt nots" were given to make us so uncomfortable with sin that when we were offered free salvation through faith in Jesus, we would be drawn to Him like a magnet.

> The Scripture declares that the whole world is a prisoner of sin, so that what was promised, being given through faith in Jesus Christ, might be given to those who believe.
>
> Before this faith came, we were held prisoners by the law, locked up until faith should be revealed. So the law was put into effect to lead us to Christ that we might be justified [pronounced innocent] by faith. Now that faith has come, we are no longer under the supervision of the law.[28]

Once a person has been drawn to Messiah Jesus, the Law has done its job. It no longer exercises its power over a Christian's life. A Christian is freed from the Law.

But that does not mean that the Law no longer applies to Christians. "The law is holy, and the commandment is holy, righteous and good."[29] Instead, we are in a completely different relationship to the Law.

The best way to understand this is to think back to the time when you were in the fourth grade learning your times tables. In school the teachers were your masters, and the lessons were strictly graded. Now you have graduated. But what you learned in school is still true, even though you are in a different relationship to the lessons. We use the times tables every day for various things, like balancing our checkbooks. But none of the fear and trembling associated with a school exam exists. The lessons that were once your master are now your servant.

So it is with the Christian and the Law. The commandments are still good, but now they serve us. They no longer condemn us before God. We learn much from them, for they show the mind of God and offer good rules for wise and healthy living.

Often parents will give their children very strict, literal rules because children have a hard time thinking in abstractions. A line will be drawn on the curb before the street and the order is, "Don't ever go past this line." The letter of this law is quite specific. But there is a "spirit" behind the order, which is the reason why the command was given. The spirit says, "The street is dangerous and we don't want you to get hurt."

But as the child grows to understand the dangers of being hit by a one-ton truck traveling at 40 m.p.h., he is allowed to leave behind him the letter of the old command because he understands the spirit behind it. He is now self-motivated to stay out of the street. The law is now "written on his heart," so he can be trusted to act intelligently. But even though he is allowed to break the letter of the law, he does not violate its spirit.

In the same way, those under the Old Covenant were given very strict, literal laws to teach them about God, themselves, and the world. But under the New Covenant, the Law is written on our hearts and the Holy Spirit shows us the spirit behind the rules. When we know the spirit of the Law, we are freed from its letter.

Many laws called for certain animal sacrifices to be made as a covering for sins. We now know that these sacrifices looked forward to Jesus who was sacrificed "once for all."[30] Now that Jesus has come and we see the spirit behind the sacrificial laws, we no longer need to offer animal sacrifices.

At times the spirit of the law is more restrictive than its letter (just as we expect a higher standard of behavior from an adult than from a child). Jesus said that the law against adultery also applied to adulterous thoughts.[31]

Under the Old Covenant there were certain foods that could not be eaten because they were not kosher (acceptable). Under the New Covenant it is legal to eat anything but, healthwise, it is not always a good idea. "All things are lawful, but not all things are expedient."[32] God's laws should not be taken lightly. They have lessons to teach us.

But what is the spirit behind the Old Covenant Law that frees us from the 613 commands? Jesus summed up the spirit of the 613 laws in two simple rules: Love the Lord your God with all your heart, and love your neighbor as yourself. All the other laws were given to show man these two great rules for successful living.

The New Covenant gives us a diploma from the Law. We are permitted, even commanded, to be responsible adults before God.

Children will often do the bare minimum required of them to be "obedient," but their attitudes betray their inner rebellion. Once they grow into adults and are free from parental controls, their real feelings come out.

Similarly, as Christians, we can never hide behind petty rules, thinking we have bought off God. The schoolmaster of the Law is gone. It is only the attitude of our hearts that stands before God.

We have graduated. We are adults.

11

Behind
Enemy Lines

In tracing how Gentiles became part of Israel's covenant program, we saw how both Jews and Gentiles become one in Jesus. This seems to throw the covenant plan upside down. Israel's uniqueness as a centerpiece of God's strategy seems to have disappeared. New Covenant believers call themselves "Christians" and join the Church. Israel is almost militantly separate from that organization. With Israel on one side and the Church on the other, have God's plans become fragmented and frustrated? How do Christians fit into Israel's covenant plan?

All Systems, "Go!"

To understand what is happening today with the covenants, we need to retrace the story just after the death and resurrection of Jesus. After the death of the Messiah, all the prophecies were fulfilled that needed to be before the New Covenant could be offered to Israel. The nation had been scattered and regathered from Babylon six hundred years before Jesus, and the sacrifice had been made to ratify the covenant. Fifty days after Jesus' death, on the Feast of Pentecost, the promised Holy Spirit was poured out in a spectacular way to show that the New Covenant was now in operation.

At Pentecost, Peter offered Israel the New Covenant with its forgiveness of sins and the gift of the Holy Spirit. But to receive it, the people had to believe in the sacrifice of the Messiah, Jesus. The sacrifice was the door to the covenant.

> "Men of Israel, listen to this: Jesus of Nazareth was a man accredited by God to you by miracles, wonders and signs, which God did among you through him, as you yourselves know. This man was handed over to you by God's set purpose and foreknowledge; and you, with the help of wicked men, put him to death by nailing him to the cross. But. . .God has raised this Jesus to life, and we are all witnesses of the fact. Exalted to the right hand of God, he has received from the Father the promised Holy Spirit and has poured out what you now see and hear.

> Therefore let all Israel be assured of this: God has made this Jesus, whom you crucified, both Lord and Christ [Messiah]."

> When the people heard this, they were cut to the heart and said to Peter and the other apostles, "Brothers, what shall we do?"

> Peter replied, "Repent and be baptized, every one of you, in the name of Jesus Christ so that your sins may be forgiven. And you will receive the gift of the Holy Spirit."[1]

Grave of Water

Baptism played a big part for someone joining the New Covenant. It was symbolic of entering into the death, burial, and resurrection of Jesus.[2] Water baptism was a way to identify with the New Covenant sacrifice—it was a perfect symbol of that covenant. Scripture often likened the New Covenant's effects to water cleaning a person spiritually, and thus a real, physical water immersion became the outward symbol of what had happened to the believer on the inside.

In the Bible the Spirit is often compared to water. Jesus spoke of the Spirit as "living water."[3] In His conversation with Nicodemus, He called an experience with the Spirit a birth of water.[4] It also is compared to water falling on—and reviving—dry, parched ground.[5] Of course these are all symbolic; the Spirit is not literally water. Baptism is an object lesson to believers. It is not the literal water that makes one part of the covenant; it is the Abraham-like faith. Yet baptism is an important, even required, ritual. It is our best New Covenant lesson.

Take It or Leave It

When Peter unveiled the New Covenant at Pentecost, he disclosed much more than the forgiveness of sins. The spiritual awakening is only the second step to an even greater goal—the coming of the Kingdom. In revealing the New Covenant, Peter also offered Israel a new age. Peter quoted the prophet Joel to explain that the phenomenon of Pentecost was the fulfillment of prophecy. Joel also had seen the coming of the New Covenant and, like the other prophets, predicted the coming of the Kingdom just after the spiritual awakening.

> . . . this is what was spoken by the prophet Joel: "'In the last days,' God says, 'I will pour out my spirit on all people. Your sons and daughters will prophesy, your young men will see visions, your old men will dream dreams. . . .
>
> 'I will show wonders in the heaven above and signs on the earth below, blood and fire and billows of smoke. The sun will be turned to darkness and the moon to blood before the coming of the great and glorious day of the Lord.' "[6]

Joel's prophecy includes much more than just the workings of the Holy Spirit at Pentecost. Joel looked forward to the end of this age. The "wonders in the heaven above and signs on the earth below" are part of the Great Tribulation to occur just before the Second Coming of Christ. These signs and wonders, which are repeated in other prophecies (especially the Book of Revelation) signal the end of the age and the soon arrival of the Kingdom Age.[7]

So why did Peter quote such a far-reaching prophecy to

explain what was happening at Pentecost, especially when so much of Joel's prophecy was not fulfilled then?

Some believe Peter was prophesying for the distant future, giving an overview of the next 2,000 years. But Peter's words show that he saw an immediate fulfillment of Joel's prophecy at Pentecost. "This *is* that spoken of through Joel the prophet" (emphasis added).

Peter's purpose in using Joel becomes almost frightening when we look at the rest of Joel's vision. The crucial thing about his prophecy is that it is conditional, meaning that its fulfillment depends upon the response of his listeners. At first, Joel tells of great destruction coming upon Israel because of her unfaithfulness to her covenant Husband. But then he adds a word of hope.

> "Even now," declares the Lord, "return to me with all your heart, with fasting and weeping and mourning. . . ."
>
> Return to the Lord your God, for he is gracious and compassionate, slow to anger and abounding in love, and he relents from sending calamity.
>
> Who knows but that he may turn and have pity and leave behind a blessing?[8]

The prophet then tells of the blessings that God will "leave behind Him," if the people repent. The blessings are conditional.

The section of Joel's vision quoted at Pentecost comes out of this list of conditional blessings. So whether Israel received the blessings and the prophesied New Age depended upon their response to the message. If they repented and accepted their Messiah, then all that Joel predicted would come to pass. The Spirit would be poured out, and this present age would end shortly with "wonders and signs." Then Jesus would return, bringing in the Kingdom. If Israel did not repent, this present age would continue.

The time of the Messiah's return and the coming of the

Kingdom depended upon Israel's response to Jesus. Peter was offering the nation its choice of futures, just as Moses had done in the Old Covenant. Israel was being offered the New Covenant, the Kingdom, and the Messiah on the one hand, or continuation under the Old Covenant and its inevitable curses on the other. It was up to them.

Later, Peter reinforced his point to a crowd that had gathered after the healing of a lame man.

> Repent, then, and turn to God, so that your sins may be wiped out, that times of refreshing [i.e., "water"] may come from the Lord, and that he may send the Christ, who has been appointed for you—even Jesus.[9]

This was not a new teaching. Jesus had also taught that the time of His triumphant return depended upon Israel.

> O Jerusalem, Jerusalem, you who kill the prophets and stone those sent to you, how often I have longed to gather your children together, as a hen gathers her chicks under her wing, but you were not willing. Look, your house is left to you desolate. For I tell you, you will not see me again until you say, "Blessed is he who comes in the name of the Lord."[10]

Ironically, the Talmud also teaches that the Messiah will not return until Israel is spiritually prepared to receive Him.

> All the [calculated] ends have already expired, and the matter [of the Messiah's coming] now depends only on repentance and good deeds.[11]

The Messiah will not return until Israel repents, accepts her Messiah, and enters into the New Covenant. The nation must be born again before it can enter the Kingdom of God.

Although many believed the apostle's message and were baptized, the majority did not. Eventually they persecuted the believers and scattered them from Jerusalem.

Because of Israel's rejection, the Kingdom could not come. Israel was doomed to continue under the Old Covenant and witness to the world through its curses, including another scattering of the nation, until God again regathered her and started the New Covenant sequence again. He has done this in our generation.

Behind Enemy Lines

Israel's unbelief blocked the arrival of the Kingdom, but many Gentiles were joining the New Covenant through Jesus and becoming citizens of the Kingdom. What was to be done with these new citizens who had no Kingdom?

The Spirit which was given through the New Covenant united them in one "body," the Church.[12] The Church was formed for all those who would become Kingdom citizens before Christ's arrival. If Israel had accepted her Messiah, there would have been no need for the Church, for the Kingdom would have come in its fullness.[13] Jesus would have taken personal command over the Earth. The Scripture speaks of the Church as a "mystery" which was not revealed until after Abraham's seed rejected the New Covenant.[14]

The Church is a temporary home for Kingdom citizens. It is like a nation in exile, comparable to the many groups of immigrants who came to America around the turn of the century. The various nationalities, feeling strange and uncomfortable in the new, alien American society, formed "Little Italys" and "Chinatowns" to preserve their culture. In the same way, the Church is a "Little Kingdom" in an alien, hostile world controlled by Satan.

Since Satan and his angels commandeered our planet, our world has been run by his rules. War, hatred, poverty, racism, and selfishness have reigned. The job of the Church is to demonstrate the contrasting life-style of God's Kingdom which soon will conquer Earth. If people want to know what it will be like when Jesus reigns as King over the Earth, they should need only to look at the Church. The essence of the Kingdom is summed up in the prayer He taught His disciples: "Thy will be done on earth as it is in heaven."[15]

God doesn't intend that we reflect the values of the society around us, but that we should bring to our society the Kingdom's point of view. Our job is to say to the world, "Look, you don't have to live in Satan's system anymore. We have a better way, based on trust and love, of building each other up, not tearing each other down." The Church's calling is to present a clear alternative to Satan's system.

The Church is an army of Kingdom citizens caught behind enemy lines. Waiting for its Commander to return, its task is to sabotage the enemy's camp.

Gentiles and Jerusalem

If Jews and Gentiles share in the New Covenant, are Gentiles heir to Israel's physical promises? Do we also inherit the Promised Land and other material blessings?

From the beginning God ordained that Israel's blessings would benefit the Gentiles. God promised Abraham that "all peoples on earth will be blessed through you."[16] Paul said the blessings of the New Covenant are "first for the Jew, then for the Gentile."[17] While the promises are directed primarily at Israel, the "fallout" reaches the Gentiles. Abraham and his nation were given certain national and spiritual promises, but Gentiles would be blessed through God's dealings with Abraham. While we Gentiles cannot lay claim to downtown Jerusalem, we do receive the blessings that the fulfillment of Israel's physical promises bring.

Sometimes the New Testament takes a physical promise to Israel and applies it spiritually to the Church.[18] This does not mean that the Church is robbing Israel, or taking over her place in God's program. All promises to Israel ultimately have an application to the Gentiles because of the pattern God established with Abraham. Because Gentiles were included in His deal with the patriarch, every blessing of Israel is shared with us in some way.

Today these blessings are not enjoyed together. But it will not always be like this. When Israel is spiritually restored, Jews and Gentiles will receive the blessings together.

The Resurrection of Israel

Israel is the key to the fulfillment of all God's plans, the key to the Kingdom. Even the Church cannot see its real fulfillment apart from Israel. Satan knows this. That is why the enemy has tried at every turn to annihilate the nation. So in a sense, we are all waiting for Israel. Her spiritual change signals the coming of the Kingdom. But the way things are going, it would seem that Israel could remain in darkness for centuries. Yet this will only make the miracle all the greater. Just as God performed an unprecedented act by gathering a nation together after two thousand years of wandering, so He will do even greater things when Israel enters the second phase of the New Covenant.

Many believe that Israel has lost any special place it may have had in God's plans because she rejected the Messiah. But the Scriptures are clear. Despite her unfaithfulness, Israel will always be in God's program. God's promises to Abraham will never fail. Israel will be God's chosen as long as the world exists.

This is what the Lord says, he who appoints the sun to shine by day, who decrees the moon and stars to shine by night, who stirs up the sea so that its waves roar—the Lord Almighty is his name: "Only if these decrees [i.e., the action of the sun, moon, stars, and waves] vanish from my sight," declares the Lord, "will the descendants of Israel ever cease to be a nation before me."

This is what the Lord says: "Only if the heavens above can be measured and the foundations of the earth below be searched out will I reject all the descendants of Israel because of all they have done."[19]

Significantly, this prophecy comes immediately after Jeremiah's promise of the New Covenant. The whole point of that contract is that it deals with bringing a disobedient nation to resurrection. Israel's blindness delays the promises, but it cannot cancel them. Because of God's unconditional agreement, Israel will be revived.

> I ask then, Did God reject his people? By no means! . . . God did not reject his people, whom he foreknew. . . .
>
> Again I ask, Did they stumble so as to fall beyond recovery? Not at all! Rather, because of their transgression, salvation has come to the Gentiles to make Israel envious. But if their transgression means riches for the world, and their loss means riches for the Gentiles, how much greater riches will their fullness bring! . . .
>
> For if their rejection is the reconciliation of the world, what will their acceptance be but life from the dead?[20]

The Apostle Paul likens the relationship between Israel and the Gentiles to branches of different trees being grafted together into the same trunk. Some of the branches (Israel) have been temporarily cut off, but since their root is in Abraham, they will be regrafted into their own tree.

> . . . If the root is holy, so are the branches. If some of the branches have been broken off, and you [Gentiles], though a wild olive shoot, have been grafted in among the others and now share in the nourishing sap from the olive root [the Covenants], do not boast over those branches. If you do, consider this: You do not support the root, but the root supports you.[21]

Christians can never feel superior to Israel. God's promises to Israel support us. Salvation is from the Jews.[22] And although Christians are heirs of Abraham, Paul issues a strong warning to us.

> Consider therefore the kindness and sternness of God: sternness to

those who fell, but kindness to you, *provided that you continue in his kindness. Otherwise, you also will be cut off.* And if they do not persist in unbelief, they will be grafted in, for God is able to graft them in again. After all, if you were cut out of an olive tree that is wild by nature, and contrary to nature were grafted into a cultivated olive tree, how much more readily will these, the natural branches, be grafted into their own olive tree?

I do not want you to be ignorant of this mystery, brothers, *so that you may not be conceited:* Israel has experienced a hardening in part until the full number of Gentiles has come in [to faith]. And so all Israel will be saved, as it is written:

> "The deliverer will come from Zion;
>   he will turn godlessness away from Jacob.
> And this is my covenant with them
>   when I take away their sins."[23]

The covenant that takes away sins is the New Covenant. Here Paul is very clear that Israel will enter that covenant. After the appointed number of Gentiles has come to faith (a number known only to God), God's favor will again return to Israel, and the nation will be reborn by recognizing its Messiah. Then there will be a joining of all the people of God—Jews and Gentiles—completing God's Babylonian rescue program. God told Abraham, *"All* the peoples on earth will be blessed through you."[24] (emphasis added).

"Shout and be glad, O Daughter of Zion [Israel]. For I am coming, and I will live among you," declares the Lord. "Many nations [lit. 'Gentiles'] will be joined with the Lord in that day and will become my people . . . . The Lord will inherit Judah as his portion in the holy land and will again choose Jerusalem."[25]

12
Raid on Megiddo

It used to be only religious fanatics who warned about Armageddon. Now it's a household word.

Armageddon is a combination of two words: *har* (mountain) and *megiddo* (Mt. Megiddo). It is a mountain in north-central Israel that overlooks the plain of Jezreel, a wide open expanse that has been the site of numerous military encounters. It seems to be ideally suited for war. When Napoleon stood on Mt. Megiddo looking down on the valley below, he is supposed to have said, "All the armies of the world could maneuver for battle here."[1] Napoleon is seldom accused of being a prophet, but that is exactly what will happen.

Mt. Megiddo is the site of the determining battle to see who will control our planet. This one event has been the focus of God's covenants since the beginning. A celestial war will be fought on two battlefields. As angelic and demonic powers struggle in the heavenlies, our world's forces will gather against Israel. The covenants have set up the final battle between God and Satan.

The plan God started with Abraham is inexorably drawing our Babylonian world into judgment. Abraham's Israel is the centerpiece of God's and Satan's strategy. To God it is the focal point of His Kingdom. For Satan it is the last obstacle to complete control of Earth.

The Adversary will move all Earth's armies against Israel in a supreme effort to solve his "Jewish problem." It is through Israel that Satan will fall; that is why he has tried so often to eliminate the seed of Abraham.

Twenty years ago the prospect of having a global war over Israel seemed ludicrous. People aren't laughing anymore. An oil-hungry world sees Israel as a stubborn nuisance, a threat to world economic and political stability. It will not be long until the nations decide that Israel must release her "outmoded" promises or be sacrificed.

Satan's war with God has been fought on many battlefields through the centuries. But those were only warm-ups for Megiddo. During the football season, two teams may play each other a number of times, but it's all in preparation for Super Bowl Sunday. The last quarter of the last game means there is no tomorrow. So at Armageddon, God and Satan are playing for keeps.

Satan knows he has an appointment with Jesus at Mt. Megiddo. Armageddon is the kind of battle imagined in mythology where wizards and conjurers are enlisted to help their armies against the enemy. Satan will use all his tools, including magic and the occult. The Bible says that Armageddon will be put into motion with the help of occultic signs performed to convince the various commanders that they have a power none of the other armies possess.[2]

An awesome example of this blending of the occult and the military is apparent today. Both the United States and Russia are experimenting with psychic phenomena in the armed forces. America, reportedly, has psychics who can discern the location of hidden bases and even read documents inside headquarters.[3] This obviously makes other forms of spying obsolete. Tragically, in the name of science and defense, the military is being drawn into Satan's backyard, hoping to get a clear edge on the enemy.

The Bad Guys

Does all this talk about wizardry and occultic miracles sound too much like *Star Wars?* Perhaps not, if we understand the man who will put Satan's Armageddon strategy into motion. Commonly called Antichrist by Christians, the Bible depicts him as "The Beast."

Coming in the role of Nimrod, he will appear to be a savior with the magic answers just as the world is screaming for someone—anyone. He will gain power through war and political intrigue and establish his state after the pattern of the old Roman Empire.[4] The war that brings him to power must be extremely disastrous because by the time he takes control, people will be willing to worship him because of his power.

> They also worshiped the beast and asked, "Who is like the beast? Who can make war against him?"[5]

As things stand today, the world would not worship a man who put an end to war. It might give him the Nobel Peace Prize five years running, but not worship. It seems the world is in for a devastating destruction before the final conflict. Satan is waiting until people scream for his miracle child.

The Bible doesn't tell us much about this man. There are hints that he may be Jewish, since he will try to pawn himself off as the Messiah, and perhaps homosexual.[6] He will arise out of what used to be the Roman Empire, which included much of Europe and North Africa, and revive that long sleeping giant. He will have almost complete world control.[7] Extremely personable like his predecessor, he will have Nimrod's ability to hold men's allegiance. But he will not be without enemies.

The Book of Revelation mentions the Beast having a "fatal wound" that is miraculously healed.[8] This seems to be his big claim to fame. After he survives an assassination attempt that should have killed him, the Beast starts believing his own press releases and demands that he be worshiped as God.

He owes much of the success of his messianic deception to a sidekick, usually called the False Prophet. The False Prophet devises a system combining religion with computer economics, where all buying and selling is done cashlessly by number, as with our charge cards today. The twist is that to receive a number which entitles one to enter the marketplace, he must worship the Antichrist.[9] As his plan has been since the beginning, Satan will be vying for the allegiance of people, making them put their money where their mouths are.

The Antichrist can get away with this kind of blasphemy because of the miracles performed by the False Prophet for his benefit.

> He [the False Prophet] . . . made the earth and its inhabitants worship the first beast, whose fatal wound had been healed. And he performed great and miraculous signs, even causing fire to come down from heaven to earth in full view of men. Because of the signs he was given power to do on behalf of the first beast [the Antichrist], he deceived the inhabitants of the earth.[10]

The marvel of fire is extremely important. It is Elijah's miracle. Elijah, who lived about 850 B.C., was Israel's most respected prophet. God performed spectacular works through him, one of which was to cause fire to come down out of the sky to prove to the prophets of Baal that Israel's God was the true God.[11] This fire sign became legendary among Israelites and the test of any self-proclaimed Messiah. Jesus was often asked to duplicate Elijah's miracle to prove His authenticity.[12]

The plot thickened around 400 B.C. when the prophet Malachi promised that Elijah would return before the "great and dreadful day of the Lord comes."[13] Elijah would be the forerunner of the Messiah.

But in the last days, the False Prophet will duplicate Elijah's phenomenon to try to identify himself as Elijah. And if he is Elijah, his cohort the Antichrist will be accepted as the Messiah. The deception is powerful. In speaking of the last days, Jesus said the false miracles would be so dramatic that they would deceive even true believers, if that were possible.[14]

The Antichrist and the False Prophet; a political leader and a religious guru. These are Satan's dynamic duo, out to win the world for the Adversary.

666

The number associated with Antichrist's name and his religio-economic system is 666. It is the magic figure that guarantees one participation in his cashless economy. Much speculation has risen over whose name fits the mysterious 666. Everyone from Henry Kissinger to the Tidy Bowl man has been indicated. But the key to 666 is found in the Bible, not *Time* magazine.

The only other time 666 is found in the Bible with any religious or political significance is in association with King Solomon, the wise king who was compromised by wealth and women.

Before Israel entered her inheritance, God laid down specific rules for a king to follow. He was not to "multiply to himself" horses or wives. Horses were forbidden because they were the military tanks of the day. The army with the most horses usually won. God wanted Israel trusting in His protection and not in Aerojet General Horse Stables. Having more than one wife was forbidden because they would lead the king and his nation into paganism.[15] Solomon promptly forgot both warnings and, in the reckless heights of his wealth and power, received yearly 666 talents or about twenty-five tons of gold.[16] Apparently Solomon was receiving Satan's salary in compensation for his sin.

This may be significant, for we can look for the pattern of Antichrist to appear not in someone who was evil from the beginning, but a good man gone bad. Later in life Solomon repented and so is not the perfect model of the Beast. Nevertheless, the parallels are intriguing.

Citizens of the Kingdom

One of today's hotly debated theological questions concerns the whereabouts of Christians during the Great Tribulation, when this world is being turned into a cinder. Will the Church endure this time of world destruction, or will it be "raptured," taken up out of the world before the Tribulation begins?

We can learn from the mistakes of the Jews in forecasting the arrival of the Messiah through Old Testament prophecies. Often events concerning His coming and ministry were combined, making it hard to see that more than one advent would be necessary for Him to complete His mission. The correct interpretation of the prophecies had to take this into consideration. The same lesson applies to the Second Coming of Christ.

Many descriptions of the return of Jesus are found in the New Testament. When compared, a disturbing fact emerges. The passages don't all agree. Some passages clearly show Jesus coming at the battle of Armageddon, ending three-and-a-half years of destruction. Life in the sea is dead. There is no drinking water, and hundred-pound stones are falling out of the sky.[17] Jesus said that if the length of the Tribulation were not shortened by God, no one on Earth would survive.[18] During that time the world will be aware of God's wrath and Jesus' soon coming, and most will be dreading it.

> Then the kings of the earth, the princes, the generals, the rich, the mighty, and every slave and every free man hid in caves and among the rocks of the mountains. They called to the mountains and the rocks, "Fall on us and hide us from the face of him who sits on the throne and from the wrath of the Lamb [Jesus]! For the great day of their wrath has come, and who can stand?"[19]

Yet other descriptions of Jesus' coming picture it at a time when the world is going about business as usual. No advance warning is given, and destruction follows.

Just as it was in the days of Noah, so also will it be in the days of the Son of Man. People were eating, drinking, marrying and being given in marriage up to the day Noah entered the ark. Then the flood came and destroyed them all.

It was the same in the days of Lot. People were eating and drinking, buying and selling, planting and building. But the day Lot left Sodom, fire and sulfur rained down from heaven and destroyed them all.

It will be just like this on the day the Son of Man is revealed. On that day no one who is on the roof of his house, with his goods inside, should go down to get them. Likewise, no one in the field should go back for anything. *Remember Lot's wife!* . . . I tell you, on that night two people will be in one bed; one will be taken and the other left. Two women will be grinding grain together; one will be taken, and the other left.[20] (Emphasis added.)

These descriptions cannot be combined; they do not refer to the same event. Can you imagine people eating, drinking, marrying, buying, selling, planting, and building when the seas are dead, the fresh water is gone, and hundred-pound rocks are falling out of the sky? Just as the Old Testament prophesied multiple messianic comings, so two arrivals of Jesus are indicated in the New Testament.

When the passages are compared, the differences become obvious. In one coming, the pattern is destruction followed by Messiah's return. Clearly, Jesus comes after the Great Tribulation has decimated the globe. In the other passages, He comes just before the catastrophe to rescue believers.[21]

That believers will escape the Great Tribulation is supported by Scripture.

For it [the Tribulation] will come upon all those who live on the face of the whole earth. Be always on the watch, and pray that you may be able to escape all that is about to happen, and that you may be able to stand before the Son of Man.[22]

Significantly, Jesus joins "escape" (from the Tribulation)

with "stand before the Son of Man." The two go together because we are to meet Jesus in the air when He returns.

> For the Lord himself will come down from heaven, with a loud command, with the voice of the archangel and with the trumpet call of God, and the dead in Christ will rise first. After that, we who are still alive and are left will be caught up with them in the clouds to meet the Lord in the air. And so we will be with the Lord forever. Therefore encourage each other with these words.[23]

At the rapture, Jesus does not stay on the Earth as He will at His Armageddon coming. He takes believers to Heaven.

> I am going there to prepare a place for you. And if I go and prepare a place for you, I will come and take you to be with me that you also may be where I am.[24]

Notice Jesus did not say, "I am coming to stay where you are." He said that we would be taken to where He is—Heaven. This "rapture" coming cannot be the same as the Second Coming when Jesus returns to set up His Kingdom on Earth. At the rapture we will be transformed as we join Jesus.

> Listen, I tell you a mystery: We will not all sleep [die], but we will all be changed—in a flash, in the twinkling of an eye, at the last trumpet. For the trumpet will sound, the dead will be raised imperishable, and we will be changed.[25]

We will join Jesus in Heaven for what the Bible calls the wedding supper of the Lamb. It will be a time of glorious and joyous celebration.[26] But we also will be preparing to join Jesus in His return to Earth, where we will take part in His Second Coming. As His army of saints, we will assist Him in setting up the Kingdom and in reigning over the world.[27]

The Good Guys

Although the forces of evil will be formidable during the Great Tribulation, God will not leave Himself without a witness. In fact there will be two. Dressed in sackcloth, one of these Old Testament-type prophets will be the true Elijah promised through Malachi. The identity of the other is unknown.[28] Their incredible powers will give them instant world recognition.

These men have the power to shut up the sky so that it will not rain during the time they are prophesying [three and a half years]; and they have power to turn the waters into blood and to strike the earth with every kind of plague as often as they want.[29]

Their task is to expose Antichrist and the False Prophet for what they are—Satan's emissaries. They will call down the Great Tribulation upon Earth. They will bring God's wrath mixed with mercy. Although the tactics of the witnesses seem harsh, God is really exercising "severe mercy." Unwilling that any be needlessly lost, He will use all possible means to shake people out of satanic delusion.

If He cannot woo them with kindness, He will shake the Earth to its foundations so that people will forsake what cannot save them. Unfortunately, man seems to seek God only when things look bad. The last time people flocked to churches in this country was during the Second World War. The Bible says that everything that can be shaken will be, so that what is really solid will show.[30]

When the testimony of the two witnesses is over, Antichrist will be given power to kill them. For awhile it will appear that Satan's last obstacle has been removed. The world will rejoice, but its celebration will be short. God will raise the two to life in final testimony to their witness.

Now when they have finished their testimony, the beast that comes up from the Abyss [the Antichrist] will attack them, and overpower and kill them. Their bodies will lie in the street of the great city, which is figuratively called Sodom and Egypt, where also their Lord was crucified. For three and a half days men from every people, tribe, language, and nation will gaze on their bodies and refuse them burial. The inhabitants of the earth will gloat over them and will celebrate by sending each other gifts, because these two prophets had tormented those who live on the earth.

But after the three and a half days a breath of life from God entered them, and they stood on their feet, and terror struck those who saw them. Then they heard a loud voice from heaven saying to them, "Come up here." And they went up to heaven in a cloud, while their enemies looked on.[31]

Showdown

With the two witnesses out of the way, the attention of the Beast focuses on the coming of Jesus. Knowing that the time is short, he gathers his forces for the greatest battle our world has ever seen. The commanders of the world's armies might not fully understand why they are fighting Israel, but the Beast's purpose is clear. He must stop Jesus' return to Earth. To that end Satan will marshal all his troops, but it will be to no avail.

At His resurrection, Jesus was given all power in Heaven and on Earth.[32] He will prove it at His return. Riding at the head of His army of saints, Jesus will land on the Mount of Olives just east of Jerusalem. The location is significant. It was from this mountain that Jesus first ascended into Heaven. Afterward angels told the disciples that Jesus would return in the same way that He left.[33] The prophet Zechariah foresaw that event.

I will gather all the nations to Jerusalem to fight against it . . . then the Lord will go out and fight against those nations, as he fights in the day of battle. On that day his feet will stand on the Mount of Olives, east of Jerusalem, and the Mount of Olives will be split in two from east to west, forming a great valley, with half the mountain moving north and half moving south. You will flee by my mountain valley . . . Then the Lord my God will come, and all the holy ones with him.[34]

The split formed by the shattered Mount of Olives will provide an escape for the Jews trapped in Jerusalem by Antichrist's forces. This time they will receive the rescue they hoped for in A.D. 70. After the Jewish people are relieved from the battle, the celestial combatants will take over.

> I saw heaven standing open and there before me was a white horse, whose rider is called Faithful and True. With justice he judges and makes war . . . . The armies of heaven were following him, riding on white horses and dressed in fine linen, white and clean. . . .

> Then I saw the beast and the kings of the earth and their armies gathered together to make war against the rider on the horse and his army. But the beast was captured, and with him the false prophet who had performed the miraculous signs on his behalf. . . . The two of them were thrown alive into the fiery lake of burning sulfur. The rest of them were killed with the sword that came out of the mouth of the rider on the horse. . . .[35]

Thy Kingdom Come

With the Babylonian world system in ruins, the Conqueror will begin building His Kingdom, following the blueprints laid down in the covenants. Jesus, the promised Messiah, will reign on the throne of David in the Promised Land, over the promised people (Jews and Gentiles), and the blessings of the Kingdom will be worldwide, as Abraham was promised.

Jesus will reign for one thousand years, a period commonly known as the Millennium.[36] The word *Millennium* is a combination of two Latin words meaning "a thousand years." Under the leadership of Jesus, this world will have the chance to become the paradise that God always intended it to be.

A theocracy, the government of God will be ideal. With Jesus on the throne, peace and prosperity will reign. Jerusalem will become the capital of the world.

Many peoples will come and say, "Come, let us go up to the

mountain of the Lord [Zion], to the house of the God of Jacob. He will teach us his ways, so that we may walk in his paths."

The law will go out from Zion, the word of the Lord from Jerusalem. He will judge between the nations and will settle disputes for many peoples. They will beat their swords into plowshares and their spears into pruning hooks. Nation will not take up sword against nation, nor will they train for war anymore.[37]

Under the Kingdom the ecosystem of our planet will be renewed. Man and animals will return to their original vegetarian diet and, because of this, the fear of man in animals will be removed. All nature will live in harmony and freedom.

The wolf will live with the lamb, the leopard will lie down with the goat, the calf and the lion and the yearling together; and a little child will lead them. The cow will feed with the bear, their young will lie down together, and the lion will eat straw like the ox. The infant will play near the hole of the cobra, and the young child put his hand into the viper's nest. They will neither harm nor destroy on all my holy mountain, for the earth will be full of the knowledge of the Lord as the waters cover the sea.[38]

The prophecies are not clear whether God will restore the protective water vapor canopy in the atmosphere that made plant life so nutritious before the Flood. Yet something must happen in order for nature to return to a vegetarian state. It is interesting that vicious animals will no longer harm man because of the "knowledge of the Lord." This may indicate an increased awareness and intelligence among animals.

One of the intriguing episodes of Genesis is Eve's conversation with the snake. Amazingly she did not say, "Oh! A talking snake!" The conversation proceeded quite normally.[39] Before man and animals were separated by fear and diet, is it possible that we could communicate with them? When humanity's original relationship with animals is restored, we may find out what our dogs and cats really do think.

Physical impairments also will be eliminated during the Millennium.

> Then will the eyes of the blind be opened and the ears of the deaf unstopped. Then will the lame leap like a deer, and the tongue of the dumb shout for joy.[40]

The physical and spiritual realms often are reflections of each other. Deserts have been indicative of the lack of water on our planet. But when Earth becomes "full of the knowledge of the Lord as the waters cover the sea," even the ground will show it.

> Water will gush forth in the wilderness and streams in the desert. The burning sand will become a pool, the thirsty ground bubbling springs. In the haunts where jackals once lay, grass and reeds and papyrus will grow.[41]

In the past the ground has born an intriguing witness to the works of God. When people proclaimed Jesus the Messiah as He rode into Jerusalem, the religious leaders protested.

> Some of the Pharisees in the crowd said to Jesus, "Teacher, rebuke your disciples!"
>
> "I tell you," he replied, "if they keep quiet, the stones will cry out."[42]

Jesus may have been speaking more literally than we suppose. At the moment of His death, Matthew records, "the earth shook and the *rocks split*"[43] (emphasis added). All God's creation felt the power of that moment.

900 Candles on a Birthday Cake

Another blessing of the pre-Flood world that returns with the Kingdom is an almost one-thousand-year lifespan for man. Paralleling Earth's restoration, man's original vitality will return. Never again will workmen feel frustrated in their daily jobs. No task will seem meaningless, for people will see and enjoy the rewards of their work.

"Never again will there be in it an infant that lives but a few days, or an old man who does not live out his years. . . .

"They will build houses and dwell in them; they will plant vineyards and eat their fruit. No longer will they build houses and others live in them, or plant and others eat. For as the days of a tree, so will be the days of my people; my chosen ones will long enjoy the works of their hands . . . .

"Before they call I will answer; while they are yet speaking I will hear.

"The wolf and the lamb will feed together, and the lion will eat straw like the ox, but dust will be the serpent's food. They will neither harm nor destroy in all my holy mountain," says the Lord.[44]

One reminder of the fallen world that will continue into the Kingdom is the snake. Although the snake will remain a lasting memorial to the rebellion, the prize has been won, the battlefield restored, and God is the Victor in the Battle for Planet Earth.

NOTES

Chapter 1

1. Job 38:5-7.
2. In his rebellion, Lucifer earned the title "Satan," "the Adversary." See Isa. 14:12-17 and Ezek. 28:11-19.
3. 2 Enoch 29:4,5; 31:3; Talmud, Sanhedrin 59b.
4. Job 38:1-7.
5. Ezek. 28:12-15.
6. Gen. 2:7.
7. 1 Cor. 6:2,3.
8. Dan. 10:4-12.
9. Isa. 37:36.
10. 1 John 3:2.
11. Heb. 1:14.
12. Eph. 3:10; 1 Pet. 1:12; 1 Cor. 4:9; Job 1-2.
13. Rev. 12:10.
14. Isa. 14:12-17.
15. Gen. 3:7.
16. Gen. 6:5.
17. John C. Whitcomb, Jr., and Henry M. Morris, *The Genesis Flood* (Grand Rapids: Baker, 1961), pp. 240, 241, 253-255.
18. Immanuel Velikovsky, *Earth in Upheaval* (New York: Dell, 1969), pp. 51-52.
19. Gen. 1:29,30.
20. Whitcomb and Morris, pp. 399-405; Gen. 5.
21. Ibid., pp. 461-464.
22. Gen. 6:3; Ps. 90:10.
23. Gen. 9:3.
24. Gen. 9:2.
25. Alexander Hislop, *The Two Babylons* (Neptune, N.J.: Loizeaux Brothers, 1959), pp. 50-51; see also Exod. 23:29,30.
26. Gen. 9:1.
27. Josephus, *Antiquities of the Jews,* book 1, chapter 4, section 1; see also Exod. 23:29,30.
28. Gen. 11:1-4.
29. Josephus, *Antiquities,* 1:4:1.
30. William Gesenius, *Gesenius' Hebrew and Chaldee Lexicon to the Old Testament Scriptures,* trans. Edward Robinson (Boston: Crocker and Brewster, 1855), p. 676.
31. Gen. 10:8,9.
32. Hislop, pp. 50-51.
33. Josephus, *Antiquities,* 1:4:2; Hislop, pp. 23, 51.
34. Midrash Rabbah, Gen. 37:2.
35. Targum Yerushalami, Gen. 10:9.
36. Cf. Jonah 1:2.
37. Hislop, pp. 42-43.
38. Ibid., pp. 50-52.
39. Pesahim 94b; Hagigah 13a.
40. Josephus, *Antiquities,* 1:4:2, 3.

41. Gen. 8:21.
42. Rev. 6:3.
43. Rev. 13:4.
44. 1 Thess. 5:3.
45. Rev. 17:1-5.

Chapter 2
1. Robert Anton Wilson, *Cosmic Trigger: The Final Secret of the Illuminati* (Berkeley, Calif.: And-Or Press, 1977), p. 21.
2. Alexander Hislop, *The Two Babylons* (Neptune, N.J.: Loizeaux Brothers, 1959), pp. 21, 22; Wilson, pp. 66-71, 81-85, 142-148; Maurice Magre, *The Return of the Magi*, trans. Reginald Merton (London: Sphere, 1975), pp. 21-24, 38.
3. Wilson, pp. 66-71, 131; Magre, pp. 7-15, 37-40, 109-128.
4. Wilson, p. 19.
5. Hislop, pp. 12, 13; Wilson, p. 143; Magre, p. 23.
6. Bhagavad Gita, 18:17, quoted by A. C. Prabhupada, *Bhagavad Gita As It Is* (New York: Collier, 1972), p. 303.
7. Kaishitaki Upanishad, 3:1,2, quoted by John Weldon and Zola Levitt, *The Transcendental Explosion* (Irvine, Calif.: Harvest House, 1976), p. 126.
8. Ibid., pp. 128-138.
9. Maharishi Mahesh Yogi, *On the Bhagavad Gita* (New York: Penguin, 1974), p. 76.
10. "Charlie Manson: Portrait in Terror," Feb. 16, 1976, Channel 7 KABC-TV, Los Angeles, 11:30 p.m.; quoted by Weldon and Levitt, *Explosion*, p. 127.
11. Gen. 3:1-7.
12. Rev. 17:4,5.
13. Gen. 8:21.
14. Gen. 11:5-9.

Chapter 3
1. J. Oscar Boyd, *The International Standard Bible Encyclopedia*, ed. James Orr, et al., (Grand Rapids: Eerdmans, 1939), s.v. "Sarah, Sarai," 4:2690.
2. Gen. 12:1-3.
3. Gen. 17:7,8.
4. John 14:3.
5. Gen. 13:14-17; 15:18.
6. The "river of Egypt" is the Nile, or more accurately, the Nile delta.
7. Exod. 23:31.
8. Num. 34:1-12.
9. Gen. 17:7,8.
10. This seems to be a common root meaning giving rise to the various usages listed by Francis Brown, S.R. Driver, and Charles Briggs (eds.), *A Hebrew and English Lexicon of the Old Testament* (Oxford: Clarendon, 1974), pp. 761-763.
11. Jer. 18:9,10.
12. Ezek. 47:13-21.

Chapter 4
1. Gen. 15:1-4.
2. Gen. 15:7-10.
3. Gen. 15:10.

4. J. B. Pritchard, ed., *Ancient Near Eastern Texts* (Princeton, N.J., Princeton University Press, 1950), pp. 353; Jer. 34:18-20.

5. Gen. 15:11,12.

6. Gen. 15:13-16.

7. Exod. 12:35,36.

8. Gen. 15:17,18.

9. Jer. 31:37.

10. Lev. 26:43,44.

11. Francis Brown, S.R. Driver, and Charles Briggs, eds., *A Hebrew and English Lexicon of the Old Testament* (Oxford: Clarendon, 1974), p. 979.

12. Gen. 17:3-8,15,16.

13. Gen. 17:17,18.

14. Gen. 17:19-21.

15. Gen. 25:12-18.

16. Thomas Patrick Hughes, "Ishmael," *A Dictionary of Islam,* ed. T.P. Hughs (London: W.H. Allen, 1885), p. 217.

17. Gen. 16:12.

18. Gen. 25:27-34; 35:9-13.

19. Gen. 32:24-32.

20. J. Oscar Boyd, *The International Standard Bible Encyclopedia,* ed. James Orr, et. al., (Grand Rapids: Eerdmans, 1939), s.v. "Sarah, Sarai," 4:2690; Francis Brown, et al., p. 979. "Sarah" is identical in form to the verb forming the root of *Israel*, but it comes from a completely different root, *sar*, meaning captain, prince, or chieftain (compare the Russian *Czar*, which is from a similar root). The name Sarah comes from the Hebrew *sar* with the feminine *ah* ending (indicating a girl). Unfortunately when it is written out, *sarah* (to persist) looks identical to *sarah* (princess), even though they are from completely different roots (Brown, Driver, Briggs, *A Hebrew and English Lexicon of the Old Testament*, pp. 975, 978, 979. This is the most respected lexicon extant).

21. Gen. 49:1-28.

22. Gen. 50:24.

23. Exod. 3:2-6.

Chapter 5

1. Mohammed Marmaduke Pickthall, *The Meaning of the Glorious Koran* (New York: Mentor, 1924), pp. 32n, 67n.

2. Ibid., pp. x, xi.

3. Ibid., p. ix; Thomas Patrick Hughes, "Ishmael," *A Dictionary of Islam,* ed. T.P. Hughes (London: W.H. Allen, 1885), p. 217; J.D. Bates, *An Examination of the Claims of Ishmael* (London: W.H. Allen, 1884), pp. 1-5.

4. Koran 2 (The Cow): 132, 133. Selections from the Koran are taken from the translations by Mohammed M. Pickthall, *Glorious Koran,* and from the translations of A. Yusuf Ali (Beirut: Printing Productions).

5. Koran 19 (Mary): 54,55.

6. Bates, *Claims of Ishmael,* pp. 1-5.

7. Koran 3 (Family of Imran):65-68.

8. Gen. 12:3.

9. Bates, *Claims of Ishmael,* p. 1.

10. Koran 2 (The Cow):135-136.

11. Koran 5 (The Table Spread):75.

12. Koran 4 (Women):171.
13. Koran 4 (Women):116.
14. Koran 5 (The Table Spread):75, 76.
15. 1 John 2:23.
16. John 5:22,23.
17. Koran 61 (The Ranks):6.
18. Pickthall, *Glorious Koran*, p. 398.
19. Matt. 24:23-25.
20. Matt. 12:36,37.
21. Koran 61 (The Ranks):7.
22. "Ayatollah Ringo Back in the Saddle," *Los Angeles Times*, Dec. 25, 1979, part 1, p. 6.
23. Joel 3:9-17.
24. Rom. 11:28,29.
25. Gen. 12:3.

Chapter 6
1. Raphael Patai, *The Jewish Mind* (New York: Charles Scribner's Sons, 1977), pp. 339-342.
2. Gen. 45:5-7.
3. Gen. 46:34; Leon Wood, *A Survey of Israel's History* (Grand Rapids: Zondervan, 1970), p. 114.
4. Exod. 19:4-6.
5. John 1:29.
6. Exod. 24:3-8.
7. Jer. 31:32; Ezek. 16; Hosea 1-3.
8. Deut. 28:1-10; Although the Book of Deuteronomy follows the Sinai Covenant by about forty years, the covenant recorded in Deuteronomy is identical to that in Exodus and Leviticus (cf. Lev. 26 and Deut. 28). The version found in Deuteronomy was quoted because it is more specific (see chapter 7).
9. Deut. 28:15-25.
10. Deut. 30:15-20.
11. Deut. 30:1-6.

Chapter 7
1. Num. 13:33-14:3.
2. Num. 14:30-34.
3. 1 Sam. 8:6-9,18-22.
4. 1 Sam. 13:14.
5. 1 Kings 10:23-25.
6. 1 Kings 10:4-9.
7. 1 Kings 4:21.
8. 1 Kings 11:4-6.
9. Lev. 26:23-33.
10. 2 Kings 6:24-29.
11. See 2 Kings 18-25.
12. 2 Kings 17:13,14,16-18.
13. Ezra 1:1-4; 6:17; 7:13; 8:35.
14. Josephus, *Antiquities of the Jews*, 11:5:2. Josephus says the ten tribes were still in Assyria "till now" (ca. A.D. 80). Jerome places them there in the fifth century A.D. in his *Commentary of the Prophets;* C.F. Keil, "II Kings,"

Commentary on the Old Testament, vol. 3 (Grand Rapids: Eerdmans, 1975), p. 421.

15. Isa. 11:11; Ezek. 37:15-23; 39:25-29; Mic. 2:12,13.
16. Lev. 26:40-44.
17. Dan. 9:24-27.
18. John 1:10,11.
19. Luke 4:14-30.
20. Mark 12:28-34.
21. Matt. 15:3-9.
22. Matt. 12:6-8.
23. Matt. 28:18.
24. John 15:24,25.
25. Matt. 12:22-24.
26. Luke 19:41-44.
27. Luke 21:22-24.
28. Deut. 28:49,50,52.
29. Nathan Ausubel, *Pictorial History of the Jewish People* (New York: Crown, 1977), p. 87.
30. Josephus, *Wars of the Jews,* books 2-5; Ausubel, pp. 87-89.
31. Deut. 28:28.
32. Zech. 14.
33. Josephus, *Wars,* 5:1:4.
34. Luke 21:20.
35. Josephus, *Wars,* 5:11:1,2; 5:13:7.
36. Ibid., 6:8:2; Walter K. Price, *Next Year in Jerusalem* (Chicago: Moody Press, 1975), p. 26.
37. Deut. 28:68.
38. Josephus, *Wars,* 7:6:6.
39. Joel 2:28-32.
40. Price, p. 26; J.M. Houston, "Palestine," *The New Bible Dictionary,* ed. J.D. Douglas, et al., (Grand Rapids: Eerdmans, 1962), p. 918.
41. Josephus, *Wars,* 6:1:1.
42. Dio Cassius, *Roman History,* 69:12-14.
43. Ezek. 20:6.
44. Lev. 26:32,33.

Chapter 8
1. Law of Justinian of 537 (novella 45); Simon Dubnov, *History of the Jews,* vol. 2 (New York: Thomas Yoseloff, 1968), p. 211.
2. Laws of Constantine of 315; Constantius (357); Theodosius (439); Jacob R. Marcus, *The Jew in the Medieval World* (New York: Atheneum, 1969), pp. 3-7; Dubnov, p. 174.
3. Law of Theodosius (439); Marcus, pp. 5-7.
4. Law of Constantius (339); Marcus, p. 4.
5. Law of Justinian (531); Marcus, pp. 6, 7.
6. Dubnov, pp. 278-284.
7. Ibid., pp. 211, 212.
8. Deut. 28:29-34.
9. Isaac Boyle, *A Historical Review of the Council of Nice* (Grand Rapids: Baker, 1973), p. 52.

10. Dubnov, pp. 178-179.
11. Ibid., p. 173.
12. Exod. 12:14-20.
13. 1 Cor. 5:7,8.
14. Rom. 11:17,18.
15. St. John Chrysostom, *Speeches Against the Jews*, IV, 1:1-4; 2:1.
16. Vamberto Morais, *A Short History of Anti-Semitism* (New York: W.W. Norton, 1976), p. 91.
17. Ibid.
18. Nathan Ausubel, *Pictorial History of the Jewish People* (New York: Crown, 1977), pp. 95, 96.
19. Marcus, pp. 137-139.
20. Ausubel, pp. 115-117.
21. Edward A. Synan, *The Popes and the Jews in the Middle Ages* (New York: Macmillan, 1965), p. 226.
22. Ausubel, p. 100.
23. Zola Levitt, *The Underground Church of Jerusalem* (Nashville: Thomas Nelson, 1978), p. 50.
24. Ausubel, p. 95.
25. Ibid., p. 107.
26. Ibid., pp. 108, 109.
27. Ibid., p. 110.
28. Ibid., p. 109.
29. Ibid., pp. 114, 115; Marcus, pp. 115-120.
30. Quoted by Ausubel, p. 94.
31. Martin Luther, "That Jesus Christ Was Born a Jew," *Luther's Works*, vol. 45, ed. Helmut T. Leheman, et al., (Philadelphia: Muhlenburg, 1962), p. 201.
32. Luther, "On the Jews and Their Lies," ibid., vol. 47, pp. 268, 269.
33. Morais, p. 154.
34. Marcus, pp. xii-xiv.
35. Ausubel, p. 99.
36. Compare Deut. 8:17,18.
37. Ausubel, p. 132.
38. Ibid., p. 233.
39. Morais, pp. 98, 99.
40. Isa 2:3,4; Isa. 11-12.
41. Deut. 28:25,45,46,62.
42. Isa. 66:8.
43. Ezek. 36:23.
44. Zech. 14:2.
45. Zech. 14:2,3.
46. Father Edward H. Flannery, *The Anguish of the Jews* (New York: Macmillan, 1965), p. xi.
47. Gen. 12:3.
48. Deut. 30:1,7.
49. Matt. 18:7.
50. Jer. 50:6,7.
51. Obad. 11-15.
52. Raphael Patai, *The Messiah Texts* (New York: Avon, 1979), pp. 90, 132, 162, 174, 175.

53. Rev. 2:5.
54. Matt. 5:16.
55. From "The Declaration of Faith" in the revised *Book of Confessions of the Southern Presbyterian Church,* 1976.
56. From a prayer given June 3, 1963, quoted by Werner Keller, *Diaspora,* trans. Richard and Clara Winston (New York: Brace & World, 1966), p. ix.
57. Quoted by Michael Strassfeld and Richard Siegel, *The Jewish Calendar 5738* (New York: Universe, 1977).
58. Ps. 129:1,2 New American Standard Bible.

Chapter 9

1. Quote by Henri Spaak, also a former General Secretary of NATO, from Norman B. Rohrer, "Belgian 'Beast' Seen as Chilling Harbinger of Last Days," *E.P. News Service* (La Canada, Calif.: Evangelical Press Association, April 5, 1975).
2. 1 Sam. 16:14-16; 2 Sam. 1:14-16.
3. Gen. 3:15.
4. Deut. 18:15-18.
5. 1 Chron. 17:11-14.
6. Ps. 2:7 (see marginal reference in NIV).
7. Isa 9:6,7.
8. C.S. Lewis, *Mere Christianity* (New York: Macmillan, 1960), p. 138.
9. Deut. 32:43 (in the Septuagint); Heb. 1:6.
10. Ps. 45:6,7 (cf. Heb. 1:8,9): Here Jehovah calls the Messiah "God." Zech. 2:10,11: Here the Messiah is speaking as Jehovah. Zech. 12:10: "They shall look upon Me [Jehovah] whom they have pierced." Isa. 44:6 (KJV): The "Redeemer" (the Messiah) is called "the Lord of Hosts."
11. Exod. 33:20.
12. Lev. 24:16.
13. John 5:18.
14. John 19:7.
15. John 20:27.
16. Rev. 22:8,9.
17. Heb. 1:6 as quoted from the Septuagint Version of Deut. 32:43.
18. From the Nicene Creed.
19. Col. 1:15.
20. Matt. 4:10.
21. Mark 12:29.
22. John 10:30-33.
23. Gen. 2:23,24.
24. Intercourse in marriage is also used as an illustration of the spiritual unity between Christ and the Church in Eph. 5:31,32.
25. Lewis, p. 142.
26. Some deny that the Hebrew *almah* (virgin) denotes a sexually virgin girl in Isa. 7:14. But when the rabbis later translated the Hebrew Bible into Greek (in the Septuagint), they chose the word *parthenos* (sexually virgin) to translate *almah.* See also Richard Nissen, "The Virginity of the *Almah* in Isaiah 7:14," *Bibliotheca Sacra* (Dallas: Dallas Theological Seminary, April/June 1980), pp. 133-150.

27. D.H. Wheaton, "Crucifixion," *The New Bible Dictionary,* ed. J.D. Douglas (Grand Rapids: Eerdmans, 1974) p. 281.

28. Ps. 22:16-18.

29. John 19:23-27; 20:19-30.

30. Dan. 9:26.

31. Talmud, Nazir 32b; Ta'anith 28b.

32. Raphael Patai, *The Messiah Texts* (New York: Avon, 1979), pp. 60, 61, quoting Talmud, Sanhedrin 97b.

33. Talmud, Sukkah 52a.

34. Zech. 9:9.

35. Talmud, Sanhedrin 98a.

36. Mark 9:12.

37. Dan. 7:13,14.

38. Matt. 26:63-66.

39. Luke 1:26,27.

40. Matt. 23:39.

41. Zech. 12:10.

Chapter 10

1. "Israeli Law: Toward Convert Control," *Christianity Today* (Feb. 10, 1979), pp. 54, 55.

2. Zola Levitt, *The Underground Church of Jerusalem* (Nashville: Thomas Nelson, 1978), p. 122.

3. "From Law of Return to Round-Trip Decree," *Christianity Today* (April 20, 1979), pp. 49, 50.

4. Deut. 30:1-6.

5. Notice how the Kingdom arrives after the regathering and spiritual rebirth of Israel in Isa. 49; Jer. 23:1-8; Jer. 30-33; Ezek. 11:16-20; Ezek. 34, 36, and 37. If the three stages are not explicitly stated, they are implied.

6. Ezek. 36:23-28.

7. Isa. 11:11.

8. Deut. 4:27-31.

9. Ezek. 37:7-10.

10. Jer. 31:31-34.

11. Ezek. 36:25-27.

12. John 3:2-4.

13. John 3:5-10.

14. John 3:14-16.

15. Exod. 16:13-16.

16. Num. 21:4-9.

17. Num. 21:8,9.

18. Matt. 26:26-28 (see marginal reference in NIV).

19. Gen. 15:6.

20. John 4:22.

21. Gal. 3:6-9,26-29.

22. Rom. 8:1; 1 Cor. 12:27; Eph. 1:3,22,23.

23. Heb. 8:13.

24. Gal. 3:15-18.

25. Gal. 3:21; 2:21.

26. Gal. 3:19.

27. Rom. 3:19,20.
28. Gal. 3:22-25.
29. Rom. 7:12.
30. Heb. 10:11-14.
31. Matt. 5:27,28.
32. 1 Cor. 6:12,13.

Chapter 11
1. Acts 2:22,23,32,33,36-38.
2. Rom. 6:3,4.
3. John 7:37-39.
4. John 3:5. By placing John 3:5 parallel to 3:6, many have concluded that being "born of water" is the same as being "born of the flesh." So "water birth" is seen as physical birth, since birth is accompanied by expelled water. While this is logical, it misses the Old Testament association of water and the New Covenant experience. That Jesus and Nicodemus were discussing Old Testament theology (and not physiology) is clear from Jesus' rebuke, "You are Israel's teacher . . . and you do not understand these things?" (John 3:10). So the correct interpretation of "born of water" must be found in Scripture. The Bible never refers to physical birth as a "water birth," but many times it uses water as a symbol of the cleansing and renewal that accompanies the New Covenant (Isa. 44:3-5; Ezek. 36:25-27; John 7:37-39; Titus 3:5). "Water" and the Spirit are clearly part of the same experience. They should not be separated. See also Zane C. Hodges, "Water and the Spirit—John 3:5," *Bibliotheca Sacra* (Dallas: Dallas Theological Seminary, July/Sept. 1978), pp. 211-220.
5. Isa. 44:3-5.
6. Acts 2:16,17,19,20.
7. Rev. 6:1-12; 8:12; Rev. 16.
8. Joel 2:12-14.
9. Acts 3:19,20.
10. Matt. 23:37-39.
11. Talmud, Sanhedrin 97b.
12. 1 Cor. 12:13; Eph. 1:23.
13. If Israel had accepted her Messiah after His death and resurrection, the gospel would still have gone to the Gentiles, as God promised to Abraham. Daniel's seventieth "week" (or last seven years before the Second Coming) would have begun soon after Pentecost. In those last years, the gospel would have been taken to the Gentiles, possibly with the help of angels (see Rev. 14:6,7). Even without the help of angels, the gospel was spread to most of the known world in the Church's first generation (Acts 17:6; 19:10).
    Had the Jews accepted Jesus, the Romans would have moved in and started the last days scenario, with one of the Caesars as the Antichrist. To show how close the end times could have been, Emperor Gaius, in A.D. 40, ordered that a statue of himself be set up in the Temple of Jerusalem and that he be worshiped as God (just as the Antichrist will do). The only thing that prevented the order being carried out was that Gaius was assassinated before the statue reached Jerusalem (F.F. Bruce, *New Testament History* [New York: Anchor, 1972], pp. 253-255).
14. Eph. 3:1-13.
15. Matt. 6:10.

16. Gen. 12:3.
17. Rom. 1:16.
18. Acts 15:15-18; Phil. 3:3; 1 Pet. 2:9 (cf. Exod. 19:5,6).
19. Jer. 31:35-37.
20. Rom. 11:1,2,11,12,15.
21. Rom. 11:16-18.
22. John 4:22.
23. Rom. 11:22-27
24. Gen. 12:3.
25. Zech. 2:10-12.

Chapter 12
1. Hal Lindsey, *The Late Great Planet Earth* (Grand Rapids: Zondervan, 1970), p. 164.
2. Rev. 16:13,14.
3. John Wilhelm, "Psychic Spies: Mind Warfare Is the Battle of the Future," *Dallas Times Herald* (Aug. 14, 1979), p. D1.
4. Dan. 7:1-7; Rev. 17:9-14.
5. Rev. 13:4.
6. Dan. 11:37.
7. Rev. 13:7,8.
8. Rev. 13:3,12-14.
9. Rev. 14:9; 20:4.
10. Rev. 13:12-14.
11. 1 Kings 18:38.
12. Luke 11:16; 9:54.
13. Mal. 4:5.
14. Matt. 24:24.
15. Deut. 17:14-17.
16. 1 Kings 10:14-29.
17. Rev. 16.
18. Matt. 24:22.
19. Rev. 6:15-17.
20. Luke 17:26-35.
21. When Jesus prophesied, He did so through the same Holy Spirit that moved Isaiah and Jeremiah and the rest of the Old Testament prophets. Just as their prophecies often combine the comings of the Messiah into a single vision, it is not surprising that Jesus' prophecies should have the same non-chronological way of combining events. As with the Old Testament prophecies, we cannot assume that the New Testament prophetic passages are in chronological order. Prophecies are usually combined in ways we would not expect. Sometimes Jesus gave prophecies of the rapture following prophecies of His Second Coming, but that does not mean that the events will occur in that order. When the descriptions are studied, the order of events as they will actually happen becomes clear. The rapture must happen before the Tribulation.
22. Luke 21:35,36.
23. 1 Thess. 4:16-18.
24. John 14:2,3.
25. 1 Cor. 15:51,52.
26. Rev. 19:6-9.

27. Rev. 19:14; 2:26,27; 5:9,10; 1 Cor. 6:2.

28. Many think the other witness is Moses, since many of the signs performed by the two are reminiscent of the plagues of Egypt. Others believe it is Enoch who, like Elijah, never saw death (Gen. 5:24). Because Heb. 9:27 says that it is appointed unto a man to die once, they believe that Elijah and Enoch must return to die. But Heb. 9:27 is only a general rule. Lazarus and all the others who were raised back to life died twice. Those taken in the rapture will never die (1 Cor. 15:51,52). It is interesting that Moses showed up with Elijah on the Mount of Transfiguration (Matt. 17:1-5).

29. Rev. 11:6.

30. Heb. 12:26,27.

31. Rev. 11:7-12.

32. Matt. 28:18.

33. Acts 1:9,10.

34. Zech. 14:2-5.

35. Rev. 19:11,14,19-21.

36. Rev. 20:4.

37. Isa. 2:3,4.

38. Isa. 11:6-9.

39. Gen. 3:1-4.

40. Isa. 35:5,6.

41. Isa. 35:6,7.

42. Luke 19:39,40.

43. Matt. 27:51.

44. Isa. 65:20-25.